Grammar: It's More Fun Than Watching Paint Dry

This is the last grammar book you will ever need

Cleave Bourbon

Shadesilver Publishing

Contents

Introduction:

This is the Last Grammar Book You Will Even Need. That may seem like a boast, but let's face it. To understand grammar for writing essays, emails, academic papers, and even novels in English you will need basic grammar knowledge and perhaps a little of the advanced stuff to set yourself above average. This book gives you all that and more. I dare say more than you will ever need.

Grammar and the parts of speech are the foundation of effective communication. There is no inflection in text. Sometimes you can't tell if someone is being sarcastic or thoughtful. In order to express such concepts in writing you have to be good at using grammar. Without a solid understanding of the rules and nuances of grammar, it can be difficult to convey your message clearly and effectively. In this book, we'll take an in-depth look at the rules of grammar and the parts of speech, providing you with the tools you need to elevate your writing and communication skills to the next level.

This book is organized into two parts. The first fourteen chapters cover basic grammar, probably more than you really want to know. Plus, I throw in some tips and tricks I have learned over the years. The second part, starting with chapter fifteen, delves into the more advanced grammar usage. Each chapter has exercises at the end of the section to help with understanding. Readers are encouraged to do the exercises after each chapter to get the full usage of this material.

Learning and utilizing English grammar is like playing a musical instrument. At first you look at the notes on the staff and coordinate with your hands and fingers where that note is played on the instrument. Eventually, with practice, you no longer think "this is an F sharp and is played this way on the instrument," and instead you see the note on the staff and just automatically go to it and play it. Grammar is the same. Eventually, with practice, you just go there without thinking about it. You place commas where they belong, use the correct noun to match the correct verb and so on. It's really that easy!

Chapter One

Sentence Types

Before we dive into the parts of speech that make up sentences, we must first understand the types of sentences. This is helpful to know for the chapters ahead.

In this chapter, we will discuss the four main types of sentences: declarative, interrogative, imperative, and exclamatory. Each type of sentence has its own unique purpose and structure.

Declarative Sentences

A declarative sentence is a statement that declares or asserts a fact or idea. It ends with a period. For example:

The grass is green.

The cat yowls at night.

I love white chocolate.

Declarative sentences are the most common type of sentence in written and spoken English. They are used to convey information or opinions. In English we usually write a declarative sentence like this: subject+verb. When a sentence is rarely written verb+subject (Learn you will.) We call that a Yoda...er... I mean an inverted sentence. The dad jokes just keep coming, sorry!

Interrogative Sentences

An interrogative sentence is a sentence that asks a question. It ends with a question mark. For example:

Are you coming to the party tonight?

What time does the movie start?

How do I get to the bus station?

When you watch a movie and the bad cop is interrogating the perp, he is asking the suspect questions. Interrogate has the same root word as interrogative. Interrogate=interrogative. It means you are asking questions.

Interrogative sentences are used to seek information or clarification. They often begin with a question word such as "who," "what," "when," "where," "why," or "how."

Imperative Sentences

An imperative sentence is a sentence that gives a command, direction, or instruction. It ends with a period or an exclamation point. This sentence has no written subject because the subject is understood to be "you" For example:

Close the door, please. ("You" close the door, please.)

Turn off the lights before you leave. ("You" turn off the lights before you leave.)

Be quiet in the library. ("You" be quiet in the library.)

Again, Imperative sentences are used to issue orders or instructions. They often begin with a verb in its base form, and the subject is implied "you".

Exclamatory Sentences

An exclamatory sentence is a sentence that expresses strong emotion or excitement. It ends with an exclamation point. For example:

What a wonderful time we had shopping today!

I can't believe we won the game!

Wow, that's incredible!

Exclamatory sentences are used to convey strong feelings such as joy, surprise, or anger. They are called exclamatory because someone is exclaiming an emotion and they end with an exclamation point.

So, that wasn't so bad. There are easy ways to remember the sentence types. Declare something = declarative, interrogate someone = ask questions = interrogative, give a command or issue an imperative = imperative (also doesn't have a written subject in the sentence), and finally exclaim an emotion and end with an exclamation point = exclamatory.

Once again, understanding the different types of sentences is essential for effective communication in written and spoken English. Declarative sentences state facts or ideas, interrogative sentences ask questions, imperative sentences give commands or instructions, and exclamatory sentences express strong emotions. By using the appropriate sentence type, we can convey our intended meaning and engage our audience.

Exercises:

1. Identify the sentence type of the following sentence: "The cat sat on the mat."

a) Declarative

b) Interrogative

c) Imperative

d) Exclamatory

2. Which sentence type is used to make a request or give a command?

a) Declarative

b) Interrogative

c) Imperative

d) Exclamatory

3. Which sentence type ends with a period?

a) Declarative

b) Interrogative

c) Imperative

d) Exclamatory

4. Which sentence type is used to express strong emotions or feelings?

a) Declarative

b) Interrogative

c) Imperative

d) Exclamatory

5. Identify the sentence type of the following sentence: "What time is it?"

a) Declarative

b) Interrogative

c) Imperative

d) Exclamatory

6. Which sentence type is used to ask a question?

a) Declarative

b) Interrogative

c) Imperative

d) Exclamatory

7. Identify the sentence type of the following sentence: "Don't forget your keys."

a) Declarative

b) Interrogative

c) Imperative

d) Exclamatory

8. Which sentence type is used to give a piece of information or make a statement?

a) Declarative

b) Interrogative

c) Imperative

d) Exclamatory

9. Identify the sentence type of the following sentence: "I can't believe it!"

a) Declarative

b) Interrogative

c) Imperative

d) Exclamatory

10. Which sentence type is used to express surprise, anger, or other intense emotions?

a) Declarative

b) Interrogative

c) Imperative

d) Exclamatory

11. Identify the sentence type of the following sentence: "Please pass me the salt and pepper."

a) Declarative

b) Interrogative

c) Imperative

d) Exclamatory

12. Which sentence type is used to express a strong desire or hope?

a) Declarative

b) Interrogative

c) Imperative

d) Exclamatory

13. Identify the sentence type of the following sentence: "The sun is shining brightly."

a) Declarative

b) Interrogative

c) Imperative

d) Exclamatory

14. Which sentence type is used to make a statement or give information?

a) Declarative

b) Interrogative

c) Imperative

d) Exclamatory

15. Identify the sentence type of the following sentence: "How are you feeling today?"

a) Declarative

b) Interrogative

c) Imperative

d) Exclamatory

Chapter Two

Phrases and Clauses

Some of the parts of speech, like prepositions and conjunctions, require an understanding of phrases and clauses, so it makes sense to understand what phrases and clauses are before we look at the parts of speech that rely on them.

Phrases and clauses are important components of English grammar. They help to convey meaning and create well-structured sentences. In this chapter, we will define what phrases and clauses are, explain the different types of phrases and clauses, and provide examples of how to use them correctly. I can't stress enough how understanding the difference between a phrase and a clause is essential to many of the grammar concepts we will be visiting later in this book.

Phrases

A phrase is a group of words that function as a single unit within a sentence. The entire phrase itself can function as an adjective or adverb for example. It does not contain a **subject** and a **verb**. It can have one or the other but not both. It does not form a complete sentence on its own. Instead, a phrase functions as a noun, adjective, or adverb in a sentence. (More on this in chapters 4 and 8) There are different types of phrases:

Noun Phrase

A noun phrase functions as a noun in a sentence. It can include an article, adjective, or preposition before the noun. For example, "the red car" is a noun phrase because it functions as a single noun in a sentence. (See chapter 4 for more details)

Adjective Phrase

An adjective phrase functions as an adjective in a sentence. It describes a noun or pronoun. For example, "the car <u>with the red paint</u>" the underlined is an adjective phrase because it describes the noun "car." (See chapter 8 for more details)

Adverbial Phrase

An adverbial phrase functions as an adverb in a sentence. It describes a verb, adjective, or another adverb. For example, "He walked <u>to the park</u>" is a sentence with an adverbial phrase "to the park." The phrase tells the reader "where" he walked. Walked is a verb and the phrase modifies it therefore it is an adverb phrase. (See chapter 8 for more details)

Clauses

A clause is a group of words that DOES contain both a subject and a verb and can form a complete sentence on its own as long as there is not a subordinating conjunction present. There are two types of clauses:

Independent Clause

An independent clause can stand alone as a sentence. It contains a subject and a verb and expresses a complete thought. For example, "She went to the store." A complete thought just means it makes sense in its entirety.

Dependent Clause

A dependent clause (sometimes called a subordinate clause) cannot stand alone as a sentence. It contains a subject and a verb but does not express a complete thought. For example, "When she went to the store." "When" is a subordinating conjunction. The clause without it would be independent and could stand alone. "She went to the store." With it, the clause is dependent on a main clause to complete the thought.

"When she went to the store" what? This clause has a subject (she) and a verb (went) but it does not make sense alone, therefore it does not have a complete thought. You need to add something to it to complete the thought. "When she went to the store, she bought milk." Now the thought is complete. What we added to the sentence for it to complete the thought is called the main clause. "she bought milk"(a sentence with a dependent clause and a main clause to complete the thought is called a complex sentence. See chapter 13)

Types of Dependent Clauses (Yeah, allow me to overcomplicate it for you!)

Adverbial Clause

Just like an adverbial phrase, an adverbial clause functions as an adverb in a sentence. It describes a verb, adjective, or another adverb. For example, "When he arrived, I was sleeping" is a sentence with an adverbial clause "When he arrived." (Tells you when I was sleeping)

Adjectival Clause

An adjectival clause functions as an adjective in a sentence. It describes a noun or pronoun. For example, "The book I am reading is interesting" is a sentence with an adjectival clause "I am reading." (Tells you what I am reading "the book" a noun.) Yes, "interesting" is also an adjective modifying the book. It's a predicate adjective. We talk about those in chapter 17.

If this confuses you a bit, don't worry about it and just move on to the next part. When you master the parts of speech, come back here, and re-read this section. It will become completely clear to you.

Phrases and clauses are important components of English grammar. Understanding how to use them correctly can improve our ability to communicate effectively. Whether we are writing an email, a report, or a book, knowing how to use phrases and clauses can help us create clear and well-structured sentences. I'll go easy on you in the exercises.

Exercises:

Identify whether the underlined portion is a phrase or a clause:

1. "<u>The man who sold me the truck</u>"

a) Phrase

b) Clause

2. Which of the following contains a dependent clause?

a) "I went to the store; I bought some milk."

b) "Because I was hungry, I went to the store."

c) "I went to the store quickly after dinner."

3. Identify the type of phrase in the following sentence:

"The girl with the red hat waved at me."

a) Prepositional phrase

b) Verb phrase

c) Adjective phrase

4. Identify whether the underlined portion is a phrase or a clause:

"<u>After I finish my homework</u>"

a) Phrase

b) Clause

5. Which of the following contains an independent clause?

a) "Although it was raining"

b) "because I went for a walk"

c) "I stayed inside."

6. Identify the opening clause in the following sentence:

"Since the store was closed, we went to the park."

a) Independent clause

b) Dependent clause

7. Identify the type of phrase in the following sentence:

"The cat in the hat chased the mouse."

a) Prepositional phrase

b) Verb phrase

c) Noun phrase

8. Identify whether the underlined portion is a phrase or a clause: "The book that I borrowed <u>from the library</u>."

a) Phrase

b) Clause

9. Which of the following has a dependent clause?

a) "I like to eat pizza."

b) "When I get home, I will eat pizza."

c) "I ate pizza for dinner."

10. Identify the type of clause underlined in the following sentence: "<u>Although he studied hard</u>, he failed the exam."

a) Independent clause

b) Dependent clause

Chapter Three

Nouns

Now we can get started on the parts of speech. The next two chapters will explore nouns. They are essential to the structure of a sentence. Being able to identify them is crucial.

Nouns are the foundation of any sentence. In this chapter, we'll explore the different types of nouns, their functions in a sentence, and the rules for using them correctly.

Definition of Nouns:

A noun is a word that identifies a person, place, thing, or idea (concept). It is often referred to as the naming word of a sentence. In simpler terms, a noun is a word that is used to name something. The subject noun is literally what the sentence is about.

Types of Nouns: common, proper, concrete, abstract, countable, uncountable, collective, and compound.

Common Nouns:

Common nouns are the most basic type of noun. They are used to name ordinary, everyday objects, people, or places. Examples include cat, bike, and town.

Proper Nouns:

Proper nouns are used to name specific people, places, or things. You can have a shoe (common) but when you name that shoe (Nike) it becomes proper. Proper nouns always begin with a capital letter. Examples include Kimberly, Los Angeles, and Pepsi-Cola. Be careful with time periods. The renaissance is common, but the Victorian era is proper because it was named after Queen Victoria of England, a real person.

Concrete Nouns:

Concrete nouns are nouns that can be perceived through the five senses. They are physical, tangible things that can be seen, touched, heard, smelled, or tasted. Examples include table, guitar, air, and perfume. Some concrete nouns may seem like abstract nouns (clouds, air) but be careful because they are concrete.

Abstract Nouns:

Abstract nouns are nouns that cannot be perceived through the five senses. They are ideas, emotions, time periods, or concepts. Examples include strength, love, happiness, time, consequences, the renaissance, and freedom.

Countable Nouns:

Countable nouns are nouns that can be counted. They have both singular and plural forms. Examples include pen (singular) and pens (plural), cow and cows.

Uncountable Nouns:

Uncountable nouns are nouns that cannot be counted. They do not have a plural form. Examples include water, rice, butter, and sugar. Although one can say I want three sugars and if they are in packets or in cubes, and can get away with it. Same thing with individual pats of butter you get in restaurants. You would probably still say I want two pats of butter rather than I want three butters though.

Collective Nouns:

Collective nouns are nouns that are singular but made up of many parts. These nouns have plurals. Examples include group, flock, herd, crowd, and army. (groups, flocks, crowds, armies) An army is made up of people, equipment, sometimes animals etc. but we call the whole (collective) thing an army. In my opinion we need to use more collective nouns. They're fun. Here are a few examples I like:

A group of owls is called a parliament.

A group of tigers is called an ambush.

A group of cobras is called a quiver.

A group of ravens is called an unkindness.

A group of crows is called a murder.

Some collective nouns you know well like:

A pack of dogs, wolves, coyotes, etc.

A pride of lions.

A gaggle of geese.

Compound Nouns:

Compound nouns are when two nouns or a noun and an adjective are put together to make a new noun. Examples include tooth+paste=toothpaste, milk+shake=milkshake, door+bell=doorbell etc. Sometimes the words are not joined together as one word but are still considered one word (or thing) such as in the compound noun water bottle.

Irregular plurals:

Words you do not add an "s" or "es" to make them plural. The plural of child is children, octopus is octopi and octopuses (also octopodes for some reason octopus has three plurals) county becomes counties. Cactus becomes cacti. By the way you can find if a word ending in "y" drops the "y" and adds "ies" or keeps the "y" and adds an "s" to make it plural by looking at the letter before the "y." If the letter is a vowel like in toy the plural is toys just add an "s." If the letter is a consonant like army, you drop the "y" and add "ies." Armies. Other irregular plurals include" knife=knives, wife=wives, mouse=mice, and goose=geese.

Functions of Nouns:

Subject:

Nouns can function as the subject of a sentence. They are the main actor in the sentence, and the verb describes their action. For example, "Sarah is singing a song." The sentence is about Sarah

Object:

Nouns can also function as the object of a sentence. They receive the action of the verb. For example, "The dog chased the ball." The ball is receiving the action of being chased.

Possessive:

Nouns can show possession or ownership. For example, "This is Sarah's book." Apostrophe S indicates singular possession as in "John's car." S apostrophe indicates plural possession as in "the Jones' house." Some nouns already ending in S but are singular nouns get the apostrophe anyway after the S as in "Melias' jacket." It's still singular possessive. It's just weird to write "Melias's Jacket." That's like saying "I and dad went fishing." It sounds better to say, "Dad and I went fishing."

Appositive:

Nouns can be used as appositives, which are words that rename or explain another noun in the sentence. For example, "My friend, the doctor, is coming over." "The doctor" is telling or renaming who the friend is. To punctuate appositives the rule is if you need the information in the appositive, you do not need commas and if you don't need the information, you do need commas. Most appositives can be removed, and the sentence still make sense like "My friend is coming over." The sentence still makes sense without the appositive "the doctor" If you need the information, we call this essential or restrictive and if you don't it's called nonessential or nonrestrictive.

Examples:

My wife, Jill, is my best friend. (Jill is nonessential because most people only have one wife or husband so if I say my wife it's going to be Jill. Therefore, I put commas around the appositive Jill)

My sister Connie has five children. (Connie is essential to the meaning of the sentence because I have two sisters. When I write my sister has five children and I have two sisters the reader doesn't know which sister I am referring to, therefore it is essential I name which sister has the five children and since the appositive is essential, I do not need to set it off with commas.)

Okay, there are a lot of things nouns can do. Nouns are an essential part of any language. They are used to name people, places, things, concepts, and ideas. Nouns come in different types, including common, proper, concrete, abstract, countable, uncountable, collective, and compound. Additionally, nouns can function as the subject, object, possessive, or appositive in a sentence. By understanding the different types and functions of nouns, you can enhance your writing and communication skills. Now, on to noun phrases. (after the exercises!)

Exercises: Write your best answer to the question (write here or on another piece of paper)

1. What is a common noun?

2. Give an example of a proper noun.

3. What is an abstract noun?

4. What is a concrete noun?

5. What is a collective noun?

6. What is a countable noun?

7. What is a non-countable noun?

8. What is a compound noun?

9. What is a possessive noun?

10. What is a singular noun?

11. What is a plural noun?

Chapter Four

Noun Phrases

Remember: phrases can have a subject or a verb but not both. If a group of words have both a subject and a verb, they are a clause not a phrase.

In this chapter, we will discuss noun phrases and their functions in sentences. A noun phrase is a group of words that includes a noun and any words that modify or describe it. Noun phrases can function as subjects, objects, or complements in a sentence.

Structure of Noun Phrases

A noun phrase typically consists of a noun, which is the head of the phrase, and one or more modifiers that provide additional information about the noun. The modifiers can include adjectives, determiners, prepositional phrases, and other nouns. For example:

The ripe **peach** on the table

A beautiful **flower** in the garden

My favorite **book** of all time

In each of these examples the head noun is in bold. The modifiers provide additional information about the noun and help to create a more detailed description.

A pre-modifier noun phrase is one that comes before the head noun in the sentence.

A post-modifier noun phrase is a noun phrase that comes after the head noun in the sentence.

Functions of Noun Phrases

Noun phrases can perform different functions in a sentence, depending on their position and context. Some common functions of noun phrases include:

Subject: A noun phrase can function as the subject of a sentence. For example:

The cat chased the mouse.

My sister is an excellent singer.

Running in the park is my favorite activity.

In each of these examples, the noun phrase is the subject of the sentence and is followed by a verb.

Object: A noun phrase can function as the object of a verb. For example:

I bought a new car.

She gave the book to her friend.

They enjoyed the concert.

In each of these examples, the noun phrase is the object of the verb and follows it in the sentence.

Complement: A noun phrase can function as a complement in a sentence, providing additional information about the subject or object. For example:

She felt <u>like a failure.</u>

The painting is <u>a masterpiece</u>.

In each of these examples, the noun phrase is a complement and follows a linking verb such as "felt," or "is."

Noun phrases are an essential part of English grammar, providing additional information about nouns and functioning as subjects, objects, or complements in sentences. We will discuss complements in more detail in chapter 19. Go ahead and try to do the exercises for this chapter. More exercises over compliments will come later in chapter 19 as well, so you should get plenty of practice.

Exercises:

1. What is a noun phrase?

2. What is the function of a noun phrase in a sentence?

3. What is an appositive phrase in a noun phrase?

4. What is a relative clause in a noun phrase?

5. What is a post-modifier in a noun phrase?

6. What is a pre-modifier in a noun phrase?

7. What is a noun clause in a noun phrase?

8. What is a complement in a noun phrase?

9. What is a head noun in a noun phrase?

Chapter Five

Verbs

Verbs are the action words that give life to a sentence. In this chapter, we'll explore the different types of verbs, their tenses, and the rules for using them correctly. We'll also discuss common errors and offer strategies for avoiding them.

Verbs are the action words of a sentence. They convey an action, occurrence, or state of being. In this chapter, we will explore the definition, types, and functions of verbs.

Definition of Verbs:

A verb is a word used to express an action, occurrence, or state of being. It is often referred to as the doing word in a sentence. In simpler terms, a verb is a word that describes what is happening in a sentence.

Types of Verbs:

Action Verbs:

Action verbs are the most common type of verb. They describe a physical or mental action. (Things that can be done) Examples include run, sing, and think.

Action verbs can be transitive or intransitive. Transitive verbs have a direct object receiving their action while intransitive verbs do not. See Chapter 16 for more detail on transitive and intransitive verbs.

Linking Verbs:

Linking verbs are used to link the subject of a sentence to a predicate noun or adjective (they tell you something about the subject and are directly related to the subject. John is a fireman. Fireman is telling you what John is. They are linked by the verb "is" John *is* fireman. They do not show an action but rather a state of being. A state of being means that you and I are "beings" human beings on this planet. I am, you are, refer to you and me as a being. Examples include is, am, and seem.

Linking verbs can look like action verbs sometimes. If you say, "She is looking out the window." "She" is actually doing the "looking" In other words the subject is doing the action of the verb. If you say, "That hamburger looks delicious." Hamburger is the subject but it's not doing the "looking" If your hamburger is looking at you something is very wrong! Since the subject (hamburger) is not doing the verb (looks) you can tell "looks" is a linking verb linking hamburger with delicious.

Auxiliary (helping) Verbs:

Auxiliary verbs, also known as helping verbs, are used to form various verb tenses, questions, and negatives. There are twenty-three helping verbs. All twenty-three are: am, is, are, was, were, will, be, being, been, has, have, had, do, did, does, may, might, must, shall, should, would, could, and can. Using different helping verbs changes the tense (time something occurs) in a sentence. For Example:

I am leaving today. ("am" indicates present tense.)

I will be leaving today. (Change the helping verbs "am" to "will be" and now it's future tense.)

Functions of Verbs:

Predicate:

Verbs are the main part of the predicate, which is the part of the sentence that describes what the subject is doing or being. For example, "Sarah *is singing a song*." In fact, you can define the predicate as anything but the subject, or the "verb" part of the sentence. I cried. "I" is the subject and "cried" is the predicate.

Tense:

Verbs can show the tense of a sentence, indicating when an action or state of being occurred. There are actually *twelve* verb tenses! The common examples of tenses include past, present, and future. We will discuss the twelve verb tenses in chapter 22.

Voice:

Verbs can be either active or passive voice. In active voice, the subject performs the action, while in passive voice, the subject receives the action. For example, "The cat chased the mouse" (active) versus "The mouse was chased by the cat" (passive). We will discuss active and passive voice in more detail in chapter 21.

Mood:

Verbs can also express the mood of a sentence, which indicates the speaker's attitude towards what is being said. Examples of moods include indicative, imperative, and subjunctive. (See chapter 20)

Agreement:

Verbs must agree with their subject in number and person. In other words, a singular subject requires a singular verb, and a plural subject requires a plural verb. For example, "The cat likes to meow" (singular) versus "The cats like to meow." (plural).

Verbs are essential in conveying the action, occurrence, or state of being in a sentence. They come in different types, including action, linking, and auxiliary verbs, and have various functions, such as indicating tense, voice, mood, and agreement. There are a lot more aspects to verbs than I could fit in this one overview chapter, so I gave many of these verb concepts their own chapter in the advanced section beginning with chapter 15.

Exercises: Some questions will require a bit of thought.

1. What is a transitive verb?
   a) A verb that does not require an object

b) A verb that requires a direct object

c) A verb that requires an indirect object

2. Which of the following is an example of an intransitive verb? (A verb that cannot have an object receiving its action)

a) to eat

b) to give

c) to think

3. Which of the following is a linking verb?

a) to run

b) to jump

c) to be

4. Which of the following is an example of a helping verb?

a) is

b) eat

c) run

5. Which of the following is an example of an action verb?

a) to walk

b) to love

c) to hope

6. Which type of verb expresses a command or request?

a) Imperative verb

b) Gerund verb

c) Infinitive verb

7. Which type of verb is used to express an action that will take place in the future?

a) Past tense verb

b) Present tense verb

c) Future tense verb

8. Which type of verb is used to describe an action that was ongoing in the past and was interrupted by another action?

a) Present perfect verb

b) Past perfect verb

c) Past progressive verb

9. Which type of verb is used to show that the subject is doing the action to themselves?

a) Reflexive verb

b) Transitive verb

c) Intransitive verb

10. Which type of verb is used to express ownership or possession?

a) Linking verb

b) Modal verb

c) Possessive verb

Chapter Six

Pronouns

No, a pronoun is not a noun that has gone pro! We use pronouns to take the place of nouns, so we don't have to repeat them over and over again in the sentence. When I was teaching grammar, pronouns were the toughest part of speech to get right for most of the basic English students for some reason. (Advanced grammar is a different story)

Pronouns are an essential part of language that replaces a noun or noun phrase in a sentence. In this chapter, we will explore the definition, types, and functions of pronouns.

Definition of Pronouns:

A pronoun is a word that replaces a noun or noun phrase in a sentence. It is often referred to as a substitute word. In simpler terms, a pronoun is a word used to avoid repeating a noun or noun phrase. (I've said that three times now. Research shows it takes three times to sink in, so you should know a pronoun takes the place of a noun by now, right?)

Types of Pronouns:

Personal Pronouns:

Personal pronouns refer to people, places, things, or ideas. They come in three forms: first-person (I, we), second-person (you), and third-person (he, she, it, they). We call first, second, and third person **perspectives.** Later, when I teach pronoun case and perspective, the perspective part means the point of view of the pronoun. (First, second or third)

Demonstrative Pronouns:

Demonstrative pronouns are used to point to or identify a specific person, place, or thing. Examples include this, that, these, and those.

Indefinite Pronouns:

Indefinite pronouns are used to refer to people or things that are not specific. Examples include anyone, someone, and everything.

Relative Pronouns:

Relative pronouns are used to link a clause to a noun or pronoun. They include who, whom, whose, which, and that. Words like "that" should be read to see if they belong in the sentence. Many times, you can just delete the word "that." This is the coffee that I like to buy. Instead, the sentence flows better like this: This is the coffee I like to buy. I call people who overuse "that" as having "that" disease.

Interrogative Pronouns:

Interrogative pronouns are used to ask questions. Examples include who, whom, whose, which, and what.

Pronoun cases:

All right, here are the keys to the kingdom. (My way of saying here is the information that will help you forever with pronouns)

I have already taught you subjects and objects when we did nouns but here is a refresher:

Subjects interact with verbs and do the action.

Objects do no action and often receive the action of the verb.

He yelled at her. (He is the subject doing the yelling. She is the object receiving the action of being yelled at.)

She told on him. (She is the subject doing the action. He is the object receiving the action.)

We call the pronoun doing the action (the subject) subjective case (sometimes called the nominative case.) And the object we call the objective case pronoun. They are not interchangeable. You will never say Him told on she. Because she is subjective case and can only be used as a subject. Him is objective case and can only be used as an object.

Knowing the cases I is subjective and me is objective. So, this is how they work:

He and she are my friends. Or They are my friends using the plural subjective pronoun.

I am friends with him and her. Or I am friends with them.

Since I is subjective and me is objective, I interacts with the verb where me does not. Dad and **I** went fishing. Would you like to go fishing with dad and **me**?

If you get confused do this:

Is it She wants to talk to John and I or She wants to talk to John and me? It's me because it is objective case. It's never She wants to talk to John and I. because I is subjective and cannot be in the objective case. That would be like saying "She wants to talk to I." If you are ever confused on which pronoun to use in which case just substitute the pronoun by itself and use it with the sentence's verb. (I want, me want, talk to I, talk to me) Same goes with My brother and me like to hang out on Saturday nights. Since me is objective and not subjective, using it this way is the same as saying "Me like to hang out on Saturday nights. Me doesn't work in the subjective case so even if you put my "brother and" in from of "me" it still doesn't work.

Let's do the plural.

Is it The principal scolded us teachers or the principal scolded we teachers?

End with the pronoun and it will become clear: The principal scolded us. (yes) The principal scolded we. (no)

Dad and I went fishing. Or Dad and me went fishing. Remove the noun "Dad" and the word "and" and just use the pronoun with the verb to reveal the correct pronoun.

I went fishing. (yes) Me went fishing. (no)

This will also clear up who and whom for you. Who is subjective and whom is objective.

Who is your friend?

"You are friends with whom?"

Possessive nouns have 's or s' while possessive case pronouns do not have apostrophes at all. Again, there are no apostrophes with pronouns. "It's" is a contraction of it is and not a pronoun. Possessive case pronouns show ownership just like possessive nouns. Some of the possessive pronouns include my, mine, ours, their, theirs, hers, his, and its.

Functions of Pronouns:

Substitution:

Pronouns are used to replace nouns or noun phrases in a sentence. For example, "Sarah loves her cat" (the pronoun her replaces the noun Sarah).

Agreement:

Pronouns must agree in number and gender with the noun they are replacing. For example, "The cat ate its food." (the pronoun its agrees with the singular noun cat. If you know the gender of the animal, you could also say The cat ate her/his food.) You cannot say or write "The cat ate their food." Because cat is singular and their is plural. The pronoun "its" never has an apostrophe (It's is a contraction of it is) It usually refers to animals you do not know the gender of like a badger. I am not about to pick up a badger to see if it's a boy or a girl. I am just going to call it an it!

Clarity:

Pronouns are used to avoid repetitive language and to make sentences more clear and concise. For example, "Sarah went to the store, and she bought some bread" (the pronoun she avoids repeating Sarah's name.)

Can you imagine repeating proper nouns like names? Sarah went to the store, and Sarah bought some bread. Sarah wanted to make Sarah a sandwich when Sarah got home to Sarah's house. Yikes!

Antecedent:

The noun that a pronoun refers to is called its antecedent. (ante means before) For example, "Sarah loves her cat. It is very cute" (the antecedent for the pronoun "her" is Sarah and for the pronoun "it" is cat).

Pronouns are essential. Without them just talking would be a laborious task. They come in different types, including personal, demonstrative, indefinite, relative, and interrogative pronouns. Pronouns have various functions, such as substitution, agreement, clarity, and antecedent.

Exercises:

Multiple Choice Questions:

1. What is a pronoun?

    a) A word that describes an action.

    b) A word that describes a noun.

    c) A word that takes the place of a noun.

    2. Which of the following is NOT a type of pronoun?

    a) Reflexive

    b) Demonstrative

    c) Abstract

3. Which pronoun is used to refer to the speaker or writer?

a) You

b) He

c) They

d) We

4. Which pronoun is used to refer to a person or thing that is not specifically named?

a) It

b) They

c) You

d) He

5. Which pronoun is used to show possession?

a) Me

b) Myself

c) Their

d) Its

6. Which pronoun is used to refer to a non-specific person or thing?

a) She

b) They

c) He

d) It

7. Which pronoun is used to refer to a group of people or things?

a) You

b) We

c) It

d) They

8. Which pronoun is used to refer to a person or thing previously mentioned or easily identified?

a) It

b) He

c) She

d) They

9. Which pronoun is used to refer to a female person or animal?

a) He

b) She

c) They

d) It

10. Which pronoun is used to refer to a male person or animal?

a) She

b) It

c) He

d) They

11. Which pronoun is used to refer to a person or thing in a place or position previously mentioned or understood?

a) It

b) They

c) He

d) She

12. Which pronoun is used to refer to the person or thing being addressed?

a) You

b) It

c) He

d) They

13. Which pronoun is used to refer to two people or things?

a) He

b) She

c) They

d) It

14. Which pronoun is used to refer to three or more people or things?

a) He

b) She

c) They

d) It

15. Which pronoun is used to emphasize a noun or pronoun previously mentioned?

a) It

b) He

c) She

d) They

Pronouns case and Perspective questions:

1. What is the subjective (nominative) case of pronouns?

2. When do you use the objective case of pronouns?

3. What is the possessive case of pronouns?

4. What is the difference between first-person, second-person, and third-person perspective?

5. How do you determine the appropriate pronoun case and perspective to use in a sentence?

Chapter Seven

Adjectives and Adverbs

Adjectives and adverbs are the descriptive words that add color and nuance to a sentence. In this chapter, we'll discuss the different types of adjectives and adverbs, their functions, and the rules for using them correctly. We'll also provide examples and exercises to help you practice using them effectively.

Adjectives

Adjectives are words that modify or describe nouns or pronouns by providing more information about their size, shape, color, age, origin, material, or any other quality that can be attributed to them. (In English grammar we use describe and modify synonymously. They mean the same thing. The red ball bounced high in the air. Red is describing or modifying ball and high is describing or modifying bounced.

Another example: "The red car is parked outside," the adjective "red" modifies/describes the noun "car" by specifying its color.

Adjectives can be placed either before or after the noun they modify. When they come before the noun, they are called attributive adjectives, and when they come after the noun, they are called predicative adjectives. For example, "a blue sky" is an example of an attributive adjective, while "The sky is blue" is an example of a predicative adjective. Yep, over-complicate it! But at least now you know.

Adjectives can also be compared using three degrees of comparison: positive, comparative, and superlative. The positive degree is used to describe one thing without comparison, such as "big," "small," "happy," or "sad." The comparative degree is used to compare two things and indicate which is superior, using "-er" or "more," such as "bigger," "smaller," "happier," or "sadder." The superlative degree is used to compare more than two things and indicate which is the highest or the most, using "-est" or "most," such as "biggest," "smallest," "happiest," or "saddest."

Note: Adjectives ONLY modify (describe) nouns, pronouns, and gerunds (since they act like nouns. See chapter 15) They do not modify any other parts of speech.

Adverbs

Adverbs are words that modify or describe verbs, adjectives, or other adverbs by providing more information about the manner, place, time, frequency, or degree of the action or quality being described. For example, in the sentence "She sings beautifully," the adverb "beautifully" modifies the verb "sings" by specifying how she sings. In fact, I personally use "how" to find the adverbs most of the time. Children often play with toys. HOW do the children play with toys? OFTEN. Often is the adverb.

Adverbs can be formed by adding the suffix "-ly" to an adjective, such as "quick" to "quickly," or by using an irregular form, such as "well" to "good." Adverbs can also be placed before or after the verb or adjective they modify. When they come before the verb or adjective, they are called fronted adverbs, and when they come after, they are called post-modifying adverbs. Most -ly words are adverbs but not all. If you self edit your writing and you remove a bunch of filter words you might not want to eliminate all -ly words. For example: The lovely flowers smell nice. Lovely is an adjective modifying flowers in this sentence and not an adverb.

Adverbs can also be compared using the same three degrees of comparison as adjectives. The positive degree is used to describe the manner or degree of the action or quality without comparison, such as "fast," "slowly," "loudly," or "softly." The comparative degree is used to compare two actions or qualities and indicate which is superior, using "more" or "-er," such as "faster," "slower," "louder," or "softer." The superlative degree is used to compare more than two actions or qualities and indicate which is the highest or the most, using "most" or "-est," such as "fastest," "slowest," "loudest," or "softest."

Some adverbs are called intensifiers because they kick it up a notch. Really and very are intensifiers and should be used sparingly. He ran fast. He ran very fast is kicking it up a notch. But, you should never do this: He ran very very very fast. That's just ridiculous! One very or one really is supposed to be plenty.

Usage of Adjectives and Adverbs

Adjectives and adverbs are important parts of speech that help to create more detailed and descriptive sentences. They provide information about the quality and manner of the noun or verb being described, which can help the reader or listener to form a clearer mental picture of the situation. However, it is important to use them appropriately and in moderation, as overusing them can lead to cluttered and confusing sentences.

BUT, despite what your writer's group says, do not eliminate all of them or trim them down too much. They add value to a sentence. Just don't be lazy and use them in dialog tags like: "He said menacingly" when you could show the guy baring his teeth and getting up close in the protagonist's face to indicate the menace.

In general, it is recommended to use adjectives and adverbs sparingly, and to choose them carefully based on their relevance and specificity to the situation. Don't over do them or go all willy nilly.

Exercises:

1. Which of the following is an adjective?

a) quickly

b) red

c) often

d) quietly

2. Which of the following is an adverb?

a) beautiful

b) well

c) happy

d) cold

3. Which of the following is an adjective?

a) softly

b) green

c) always

d) fast

4. Which of the following is an adverb?

a) intelligent

b) quickly

c) pretty

d) small

5. Which of the following is an adjective?

a) silently

b) ugly

c) softly

d) slowly

6. Which of the following is an adverb?

a) important

b) easily

c) big

d) nice

7. Which of the following is an adjective?

a) well

b) brown

c) beautifully

d) always

8. Which of the following is an adverb?

a) tiny

b) carefully

c) interesting

d) fantastic

9. Which of the following is an adjective?

a) kindly

b) old

c) loudly

d) warmly

10. Which of the following is an adverb?

a) happy

b) slowly

c) blue

d) energetic

11. Which of the following is an adjective?

a) badly

b) friendly

c) quietly

d) nicely

12. Which of the following is an adverb?

a) beautiful

b) quickly

c) young

d) huge

13. Which of the following is an adjective?

a) hard

b) quickly

c) angrily

d) carefully

14. Which of the following is an adverb?

a) funny

b) always

c) kind

d) easily

15. Which of the following is an adjective?

a) happily

b) hot

c) slowly

d) long

16. Which of the following is an adverb?

a) delicious

b) honestly

c) tall

d) pretty

17. Which of the following is an adjective?

a) softly

b) new

c) gently

d) loudly

18. Which of the following is an adverb?

a) dark

b) quickly

c) beautiful

d) interesting

19. Which of the following is an adjective?

a) quickly

b) cold

c) silently

d) hard

20. Which of the following is an adverb?

a) friendly

b) always

c) small

d) well

Chapter Eight

Adjective and Adverb Phrases

In English, adjectives and adverbs are essential parts of speech that modify or describe nouns, pronouns, verbs, adjectives, or other adverbs. Adjective and adverb phrases are groups of words that function as a single part of speech and serve to modify or describe other words in a sentence. In this chapter, we will explore the nature and use of adjective and adverb phrases in English grammar.

Remember: Phrases act as a single unit in the sentence and do not contain both a subject and a verb. They can have one or the other but not both.

Adjective Phrases

An adjective phrase is a group of words that modify a noun or pronoun in a sentence. It consists of an adjective and any modifiers that further describe or specify the adjective. For example:

The big, black cat with green eyes

In this example, "big" is the adjective, and "black" and "with green eyes" are modifiers that further describe the cat. Together, they form the adjective phrase "big, black cat with green eyes."

Adjective phrases can occur before or after the noun they modify. When an adjective phrase occurs before the noun, it is known as an attributive adjective phrase, and when it occurs after the noun, it is known as a predicate adjective phrase. For example:

The shiny silver car (attributive)

The car is shiny and silver. (predicate)

Adjective phrases can also function as complements or appositives. In these cases, they are not modifying a noun, but rather completing the meaning of the sentence. For example:

She was happy with her new job.

Although an adjective cannot modify another adjective, an adjective phrase can modify an adjective.

Adverb Phrases

An adverb phrase is a group of words that modifies a verb, adjective, or another adverb in a sentence. It consists of an adverb and any modifiers that further describe or specify the adverb. For example:

He walked slowly and cautiously down the dark hallway.

In this example, "slowly" and "cautiously" are adverbs, and together they form the adverb phrase "slowly and cautiously." Slowly and cautiously is how he walked. Walked is a verb so the entire phrase is the adverb describing how he walked.

Adverb phrases can occur in different positions in a sentence. They can occur before the verb, after the verb, or at the beginning or end of a sentence. An adverb phrase can even modify the entire sentence. For example:

He quickly ate his breakfast before leaving for work. (before the verb)

She sang beautifully as she played the piano. (after the verb)

In the morning, he always goes for a run. (at the beginning of the sentence)

They arrived at the party late, as usual. (at the end of the sentence)

Adverb phrases can also function as complements or modifiers. In these cases, they are not modifying a verb, but rather completing the meaning of the sentence. For example:

The children played in the park <u>for hours</u>. For hours is how long the children played.

He slept <u>through the entire movie</u>. Through the entire movie what he slept though.

Differences Between Adjective and Adverb Phrases

The main difference between adjective and adverb phrases is the part of speech they modify. Adjective phrases modify nouns and pronouns, while adverb phrases modify verbs, adjectives, or other adverbs. Additionally, adjective phrases usually occur before or after the noun they modify, while adverb phrases can occur in various positions in a sentence.

Another difference is the structure of the phrases themselves. Adjective phrases always begin with an adjective, while adverb phrases begin with an adverb, but can also include additional modifiers such as prepositional phrases or infinitive phrases.

Exercises:

1. What is an adjective phrase?

a) A group of words that modify a verb

b) A group of words that modify a noun or pronoun

c) A group of words that modify an adverb

2. What is an adverb phrase?

a) A group of words that modify a noun

b) A group of words that modify a verb, adjective, or another adverb

c) A group of words that modify a pronoun

3. Which of the following is an example of an adjective phrase?

a) The dog ran quickly

b) The car with the broken window

c) The boy spoke loudly

4. Which of the following is an example of an adverb phrase?

a) The book on the table

b) The girl with the red hair

c) The dog barked loudly

5. What is the function of an adjective phrase in a sentence?

a) To modify a verb

b) To modify a noun or pronoun

c) To modify an adverb

6. What is the function of an adverb phrase in a sentence?

a) To modify a noun

b) To modify a verb, adjective, or another adverb

c) To modify a pronoun

7. Can a prepositional phrase be used as an adjective phrase?

a) Yes

b) No

8. Can a prepositional phrase be used as an adverb phrase?

a) Yes

b) No

9. What is the difference between an adjective phrase and an adverb phrase?

a) An adjective phrase modifies a verb, while an adverb phrase modifies a noun or pronoun.

b) An adjective phrase modifies a noun or pronoun, while an adverb phrase modifies a verb, adjective, or another adverb.

c) An adjective phrase modifies a pronoun, while an adverb phrase modifies a preposition.

10. Can an adverb phrase modify a noun?

a) Yes

b) No

11. Can an adjective phrase modify a verb?

a) Yes

b) No

12. Can an adjective phrase modify another adjective?

a) Yes

b) No

13. Can an adverb phrase modify a preposition?

a) Yes

b) No

14. Can an adverb phrase modify a noun clause?

a) Yes

b) No

15. Can an adverb phrase modify an entire sentence?

a) Yes

b) No

Chapter Nine

Prepositions

Prepositions are an important part of speech that connects nouns or pronouns to other words in a sentence. They indicate the relationship between the object of the preposition and other elements of the sentence, such as the subject, verb, or another noun. In other words, they show a relationship between two nouns.

A preposition is usually placed before a noun or pronoun to form a prepositional phrase, which consists of the preposition, the object of the preposition, and any modifiers of the object. For example, in the sentence "The book is on the table," the preposition "on" connects the object "table" to the subject "book."

Or even in more simple terms, on is telling you where in space the book is located in relation to the table. It's on it.

Common Prepositions

There are many prepositions in English, but some of the most common ones include:

About, Above, Across, After, Against, Along, Among, Around, At, Before, Behind, Below, Beneath, Beside,

Between, Beyond, By, Down, During, Except, For, From, In, Inside, Into, Like, Near, Of, Off, On, Out,

Outside, Over, Past, Since, Through, Throughout, To, Toward, Under, Until, Up, Upon, With, Within,

Without.

Usage of Prepositions

Prepositions are used in a variety of ways to indicate different relationships between elements of a sentence. Some common uses of prepositions include:

Time:

Prepositions can be used to indicate the time at which something happens, such as "in," "on," "after," "during," "before," or "at." For example, "I will meet you <u>at 3 PM</u>," or "The party is <u>on Saturday</u>."

Location:

Prepositions can be used to indicate the location of something, such as "in," "on," "at," "by," or "near." For example, "The store is <u>on Main Street</u>," or "The cat is <u>under the table</u>." The prepositions are on and under and the underlined is the whole phrase. The noun at the end of the phrase is the object of the preposition.

Direction:

Prepositions can be used to indicate the direction of movement, such as "to," "from," "toward," or "away from." For example, "She walked to the store," or "He ran away from the danger."

Relationship:

Prepositions can be used to indicate a relationship between two things, such as "of," "with," or "for." For example, "The love of a mother for her child is unconditional," or "I am grateful for your help," "This is the sugar for the cake."

Comparison:

Prepositions can be used to indicate a comparison between two things, such as "like" or "than." For example, "She runs like a cheetah," or "He is taller than his brother."

It is important to use prepositions appropriately and accurately to convey the intended meaning of a sentence. Prepositions can sometimes be tricky to use correctly.

Punctuating a prepositional phrase:

The rule of thumb is that if a prepositional phrase appears anywhere in the sentence besides the opening phrase there is no comma; however, if the prepositional phrase **opens** a sentence and it is longer than **three** words or if there are two phrases together there should be a comma after the phrase or phrases. For Example:

At the end of a long day, I like to relax. "At the end" and "of a long day" are two prepositional phrases together. Put a comma after the second one.

"Over the Rocky Mountains, we traveled." The opening prepositional phrase has more than three words, so a comma is placed after mountains. "Over the mountains we traveled." would not have a comma because the opening prepositional phrase is only three words.

After the rain the air smelled fresh. After the rain is a phrase only three words long so no comma is needed.

Prepositions, specifically ending a sentence with a preposition is another one of those controversial topics in English grammar. When I am writing (except in dialogue where anything goes) I try not to end a sentence with a preposition. When speaking I don't even think about it. If you overhear an argument, you might say to your friend standing next to you: "What was all that about?" "About" is a preposition, and I don't see anything wrong with ending that particular sentence with it. I would say avoid ending sentences with a preposition in writing especially academic writing just to be safe.

Exercises:

1. Prepositions:

1. I will meet you _________ the library.
A.) at
B.) on
C.) in
D.) under
2. The ball is _________ the box.
A.) over

B.) beside

C.) in

D.) between

3. She was sitting _________ the couch.

A.) at

B.) on

C.) in

D.) above

4. The cat is sleeping _________ the chair.

A.) under

B.) beside

C.) on

D.) between

5. We will arrive _________ the airport at 8 PM.

A.) on

B.) in

C.) at

D.) under

6. The school is _________ the hospital and the park.

A.) between

B.) over

C.) under

D.) through

7. The vase is _________ the table.

A.) beside

B.) on

C.) under

D.) between

8. The keys are _________ the drawer.

A.) in

B.) on

C.) above

D.) behind

9. She lives _________ her parents.

A.) with

B.) in

C.) on

D.) under

10. The dog is hiding _________ the bed.

A.) in

B.) on

C.) over

D.) beside

1. **Prepositions and Antecedents:**

1. Which of the following is an example of a preposition?

A.) dog

B.) under

C.) happy

D.) car

2. Which of the following is the correct use of a preposition?

A.) They went to the movies with she.

B.) He gave the gift to him and I.

C.) She stood beside her friend.

D.) The dog chased the ball in him.

3. Which of the following is the antecedent of this sentence? The cat cleaned its tail.

A.) cat

B.) tail

C.) cleaned

D.) its

4. Which of the following is a correct use of an antecedent?

A.) He said that they would meet at the park, but it was too hot.

B.) She gave her friend the bracelet, and she loved it.

C.) The car needed new tires, so it went to the mechanic.

D.) The students were told they had a test the next day.

5. Which of the following is a preposition that can indicate location?

A.) between

B.) for

C.) until

D.) above

6. Which of the following is an example of a correct pronoun-antecedent agreement?

A.) Everyone forgot their books at home.

B.) Students should bring his or her own calculator.

C.) The team celebrated its victory with a pizza party.

D.) The employees requested their paychecks be delivered early.

7. Which of the following is a correct use of a pronoun-antecedent agreement?

A.) Neither the dog nor the cat would eat their food.

B.) Either my sister or my brother will bring their car.

C.) Everyone in the room should raise their hand.

D.) The children didn't want to do their homework.

8. Which of the following is an antecedent that refers to a person?

A.) The book

B.) The car

C.) The dog

D.) The teacher

9. Which of the following is the correct use of a preposition to show movement?

A.) She jumped in the bed.

B.) He walked on the street.

C.) They swam above the water.

D.) The bird flew between the trees.

Chapter Ten

Conjunctions

Conjunctions are an important part of speech that connect words, phrases, or clauses within a sentence. They help to clarify the relationships between different parts of a sentence and to make our writing more coherent and cohesive. The Latin root word "junct" literally means join.

Types of Conjunctions

There are three main types of conjunctions: coordinating conjunctions, subordinating conjunctions, and correlative conjunctions.

Coordinating Conjunctions:

Coordinating conjunctions connect two independent clauses, or two equal sentence elements. They are used to join two ideas of equal importance, and include the following:

For

And

Nor

But

Or

Yet

So

If you notice the bolded letters, you can remember all seven coordinating conjunctions easily as FANBOYS.

Two independent clauses connected by a coordinating conjunction is called a compound sentence.

For example: "She wanted to go to the store, but it was raining outside." She wanted to go to the store. Is an independent clause, and It was raining outside. is an independent clause.

You could also join these two sentences with a semicolon. She wanted to go to the store: it was raining outside. You just can't combine them with a comma because that would be a comma splice. Commas cannot be used to combine two independent clauses.

Subordinating Conjunctions:

Subordinating conjunctions connect an independent clause with a dependent clause (sometimes called a subordinate clause), or a sentence element that cannot stand alone as a complete sentence. They indicate a relationship of dependence between the two clauses and include the following:

After, Although, As, Because, Before, Even though, If, Since, That, Unless, Until, When, Where, While

For example: "I will go for a walk <u>after I finish my work</u>."

But wait a second! In the last chapter on prepositions, I told you after, before, since, and other words were prepositions. How can they now be subordinating conjunctions? Simple, if they are used with a phrase, they are prepositions: after it rains, before it snows, since yesterday, until noon. Etc. If they are used with a clause, they are subordinate conjunctions: After you go the store, before you arrived, since you asked, until I failed. Remember a clause has both a subject and a verb: You go, you arrived, you asked, I failed. Etc.

Correlative Conjunctions: Correlative conjunctions are used in pairs to connect two equal sentence elements, such as nouns, verbs, or adjectives. They include the following pairs:

Both/and

Either/or

Neither/nor

Not only/but also

Whether/or

For example: "She is not only smart but also kind."

Usage of Conjunctions

Conjunctions are used to join words, phrases, and clauses within a sentence, and to show the relationship between them. They can be used in a variety of ways, including:

Coordinating Conjunctions:

Coordinating conjunctions are used to join two independent clauses or two equal sentence elements. They can also be used to join words, phrases, or clauses of the same type.

Subordinating Conjunctions:

Subordinating conjunctions are used to join an independent clause with a dependent clause. They can indicate the cause, effect, time, or condition of the action in the dependent clause. They do not join words or phrases, just clauses. Independent clauses joined together with dependent clauses with a subordinating conjunction are called complex sentences.

Correlative Conjunctions:

Correlative conjunctions are used to join two equal sentence elements, such as nouns, verbs, or adjectives. They are always used in pairs and are placed before each sentence element.

Conjunctions don't have to be difficult. With a little practice, they are easy to master.

Exercises:

Coordinating Conjunctions:

1. Which of the following is a coordinating conjunction?
   a) because
   b) although
   c) and
   d) since

   2. Which coordinating conjunction is used to express a contrast or opposition?
   a) and
   b) but

c) or

d) so

3. Which coordinating conjunction is used to express a choice between two options?

a) and

b) but

c) or

d) so

4. Which coordinating conjunction is used to express a reason or cause?

a) and

b) but

c) or

d) for

5. Which coordinating conjunction is used to express a result or consequence?

a) and

b) but

c) or

d) so

6. Which coordinating conjunction is used to express a condition?

a) and

b) but

c) or

d) if

7. Which coordinating conjunction is used to express a continuation or addition?

a) and

b) but

c) or

d) so

8. Which coordinating conjunction is used to express a comparison?

a) and

b) but

c) or

d) as

9. Which coordinating conjunction is used to express a concession or contrast?

a) and

b) but

c) or

d) yet

10. Which coordinating conjunction is used to express a purpose?

a) and

b) but

c) or

d) for

Subordinating Conjunctions:

1. Which of the following is a subordinating conjunction?

A) and

B) because

C) nor

D) both A and C

2. What does a subordinating conjunction do in a sentence?

A) connects two independent clauses

B) introduces a dependent clause

C) adds emphasis to a sentence

D) none of the above

3. Which of the following is a subordinating conjunction that shows time?

A) although

B) since

C) before

D) but

4. Which of the following is a subordinating conjunction that shows contrast?

A) however

B) because

C) yet

D) both A and C

5. Which subordinating conjunction is used to show cause and effect?

A) although

B) unless

C) therefore

D) neither A nor B

6. Which subordinating conjunction is used to show purpose?

A) since

B) in order that

C) even though

D) both A and C

7. Which subordinating conjunction is used to show condition?

A) unless

B) although

C) both A and B

D) neither A nor B

8. Which of the following sentences uses a subordinating conjunction correctly?

A) I will go to the store, and I will buy some milk.

B) Because it was raining, we decided to cancel the picnic.

C) She ate dinner, she watched a movie.

D) None of the above

9. Which of the following subordinating conjunctions shows a comparison?

A) as

B) since

C) unless

D) both B and C

10. Which of the following sentences uses a subordinating conjunction incorrectly?

A) Although he was sick, he still went to work.

B) I will go to the store after I finish my homework.

C) Because she was hungry, she decided to take a nap.

D) All of the Above

Correlative Conjunctions:

1. What are correlative conjunctions?

A) They are conjunctions that connect two independent clauses

B) They are conjunctions that connect a dependent clause to an independent clause

C) They are pairs of conjunctions that work together to connect sentence elements

D) None of the above

2. Which of the following is a correlative conjunction?

A) and

B) because

C) either...or

D) both A and B

3. What is the purpose of using correlative conjunctions?

A) To add emphasis to a sentence

B) To connect two independent clauses

C) To show cause and effect

D) To connect two sentence elements that have equal importance

4. Which of the following correlative conjunctions is used to show a contrast?

A) neither...nor

B) both...and

C) either...or

D) not only...but also

5. Which of the following sentences uses a correlative conjunction correctly?

A) Either you come with me, or I will go alone.

B) Not only I like pizza, but my sister likes it too.

C) Neither my mom nor my dad can speak French.

D) Both A and C

Chapter Eleven

Interjections

Interjections are short exclamations or expressions of emotion that are often used to convey a speaker's feelings or attitudes towards a particular situation or event. They are not grammatically connected to the rest of the sentence, but rather stand alone as independent words or phrases before the beginning of the sentence. They should not be used with academic writing, but they are nearly essential to creative writing and dialogue. If the emotion is strong, they are punctuated with a exclamation point, a comma if the feeling is not as strong.

Types of Interjections

Interjections come in a variety of forms and can be classified into several different categories based on their meaning or usage. Some common types of interjections include:

Expressions of surprise or shock:

Oh! Wow! Yikes! Ouch! Holy cow!

Expressions of joy or happiness:

Yay! Hooray! Bravo! Woohoo! Awesome!

Expressions of disgust or disapproval:

Ugh! Gross! Blech! Yuck! Ew!

Expressions of agreement or acknowledgement:

Yes! Okay! Alright! Indeed! Absolutely!

Usage of Interjections

Interjections can be used in a variety of ways, depending on the speaker's intention or purpose. Some common uses of interjections include:

Expressing emotions or reactions: Interjections are often used to express a speaker's emotions or reactions to a particular situation or event. For example, "Oh no! I forgot my keys!" conveys the speaker's sense of disappointment or frustration at having forgotten their keys.

Adding emphasis: Interjections can also be used to add emphasis or emphasis to a statement or sentence. For example, "Wow, that was an incredible performance!" conveys the speaker's sense of amazement or admiration.

Introducing a statement or idea: Interjections can also be used to introduce a statement or idea, particularly in informal or conversational contexts. For example, "Hey, did you hear about the new restaurant that just opened?" serves as an introduction to the speaker's statement about the new restaurant. Be sure not to overuse when writing creatively.

It is important to note that while interjections can add color and emotion to language, they should be used sparingly and appropriately. There really isn't much to remember rule-wise about this part of speech. It's easy to punctuate (Exclamation if the emotion is strong, a comma if the emotion is weaker) and it's easy to spot when editing. However, the overuse of interjections can make writing or speech seem unprofessional or juvenile. If you noticed in the examples above interjections tend to be used almost exclusively in dialogue good for you!

Exercises:

1. What is an interjection?

a) A type of sentence

b) A part of speech

c) A form of punctuation

2. Which of the following is an example of an interjection?

a) The cat jumped over the fence

b) Wow!

c) I am going to the store

3. Which of the following interjections expresses surprise?

a) Hurray!

b) Oops!

c) Wow!

4. Which of the following interjections expresses agreement?

a) Ugh!

b) Yeah!

c) Oops!

5. Which of the following interjections expresses disapproval?

a) Yay!

b) Oh no!

c) Ahem!

6. Which of the following interjections is used to get someone's attention?

a) Oh no!

b) Ahem!

c) Hurray!

7. Which of the following interjections is used to express relief?

a) Hurray!

b) Phew!

c) Oops!

8. Which of the following interjections is used to express happiness?

a) Ugh!

b) Yay!

c) Oops!

9. Which of the following interjections is used to express sympathy?

a) Oops!

b) Aww!

c) Yay!

10. Which of the following interjections is used to express anger?

a) Oh no!

b) Ugh!

c) Yay!

11. Which of the following interjections is used to express excitement?

a) Oops!

b) Yay!

c) Ahem!

12. Which of the following interjections is used to express doubt?

a) Hmm...

b) Yay!

c) Oops!

13. Which of the following interjections is used to express frustration?

a) Oops!

b) Ugh!

c) Yay!

14. Which of the following interjections is used to express admiration?

a) Wow!

b) Ugh!

c) Phew!

15. Which of the following interjections is used to express gratitude?

a) Oops!

b) Thank you!

c) Ahem!

Chapter Twelve

Articles

In English, articles are words that come before a noun to indicate its specificity or generalization. There are two types of articles: definite and indefinite. These used to be called article adjectives but somewhere, somehow they got promoted to the ninth part of speech.

Indefinite Articles

Indefinite articles refer to non-specific or unidentified nouns. The two indefinite articles in English are "a" and "an." "a" is used before a singular noun that begins with a consonant sound, while "an" is used before a singular noun that begins with a vowel sound. Note: I said consonant SOUND and vowel SOUND, not the first letter of the noun that follows. Words like "hour" for example begin with a consonant but have a vowel sound, so this word "hour" gets "an" rather than "a." "I'll be there in an hour."

The word Opossum is controversial. Some pronounce it with the "O" and some do not. If you pronounce the "O" use "an" and if you pronounce it "possum" then use "a."

Examples of article usage:

A cat

An apple

A book

An umbrella

An hour (Remember: it isn't the letter the word starts with but rather the sound the word makes)

Definite Articles:

Definite articles refer to specific nouns that have already been mentioned or are easily identifiable. The definite article in English is "the."

For example:

The cat

The apple

The book

The umbrella

The hour

When to Use Articles

The use of articles depends on the context and the noun being referred to. Here are some guidelines:

Use "a" or "an" when referring to a singular, non-specific noun. For example, "I saw a dog on the street."

Use "the" when referring to a specific noun that has already been mentioned or is easily identifiable. For example, "I saw a dog on the street. The dog was brown and fluffy."

Use "the" when referring to a specific noun that is unique or one-of-a-kind. For example, "The Eiffel Tower is in Paris."

Use "a" or "an" when referring to a singular, countable noun that is part of a group. For example, "I ate an apple from the basket."

Use "the" when referring to a plural noun that is specific. For example, "I saw the cats playing in the garden."

Use no article when referring to a non-countable noun that is being used in a general sense. For example, "I like coffee." But you can use "the" with a non-countable noun like this: "Pass me the butter."

Exercises:

1. Which of the following is NOT an article?

    a) a

    b) an

    c) the

    d) none of the above

2. Which article is used before a vowel sound?

    a) a

    b) an

    c) the

    d) None of the Above

3. Which article is used before a singular countable noun that is specific or particular?

    a) a

    b) an

    c) the

    d) None of the Above

4. Which article is used before a singular countable noun that is not specific or particular?

    a) a

    b) an

c) the

d) None of the Above

5. Which article is used before a plural countable noun that is specific or particular?

a) a

b) an

c) the

d) None of the Above

6. Which article is used before an uncountable noun?

a) a

b) an

c) the

d) none

7. Which of the following sentences uses the indefinite article correctly?

a) I need the apple

b) I need an apple

c) I need apple

d) None of the Above

8. Which of the following sentences uses the definite article correctly?

a) A cat is on the roof

b) The cat is on the roof

c) Cat is on the roof

d) None of the Above

9. Which of the following sentences uses the indefinite article correctly?

a) The book is interesting

b) A book is interesting

c) Book is interesting

d) None of the Above

10. Which of the following sentences uses the definite article correctly?

a) I saw a lion at the zoo

b) I saw lion at the zoo

c) I saw the lion at the zoo

d) None of the Above

11. Which of the following sentences uses the indefinite article correctly?

a) I am going to the school

b) I am going to a school

c) I am going to school

d) None of the Above

12. Which of the following sentences uses the definite article correctly?

a) A dog chased me yesterday

b) The dog chased me yesterday

c) Dog chased me yesterday

d) None of the Above

13. Which of the following sentences uses the indefinite article correctly?

a) He is playing the guitar

b) He is playing a guitar

c) He is playing guitar

d) None of the Above

14. Which of the following sentences uses the definite article correctly?

a) I like a pizza with extra cheese

b) I like pizza with extra cheese

c) I like the pizza with extra cheese

d) None of the Above

15. Which of the following sentences uses the indefinite article correctly?

a) I am going to the movie

b) I am going to a movie

c) I am going to movie

d) None of the Above

Chapter Thirteen

Sentence Structure

Sentence structure is the arrangement of words, phrases, and clauses to create meaningful sentences. In English, a basic sentence consists of a subject, a verb, and an object usually in that order. However, sentence structure can be more complex, depending on the type of sentence being used.

Simple Sentences

A simple sentence is a sentence that consists of a single independent clause. An independent clause contains a subject and a predicate. It can stand alone as a complete sentence. Simple means they are not complicated. Sible sentences can contain compound subjects and predicates and still be simple. For example:

The German shepherd and Doberman pinscher barked. (compound subject)

She hums and sings beautifully. (compound predicate or compound verb if you wish)

The sun rises in the east.

Compound Sentences

A compound sentence consists of two or more independent clauses that are joined by a **coordinating** conjunction, such as "and," "but," or "or." If you remove the conjunction, you have two simple sentences. You can also join two independent clauses with a semicolon. For example:

I like to read books, but my sister prefers to watch movies.

The sky was blue, and the sun was shining. With semicolon: The sky was blue; the sun was shining.

He went to the store, and she stayed home.

Complex Sentences

A complex sentence consists of one independent clause and at least one dependent (subordinate) clause, which cannot stand alone as a complete sentence. Dependent clauses begin with subordinating conjunctions, such as "because," "although," or "since." For example:

Although it was raining, we decided to go for a walk.

Because I was tired, I went to bed early. (comma after dependent clause) Also: I went to bed early because I was tired. (no comma)

Since she missed the bus, she had to walk to school. (comma after dependent clause) Also: She had to walk to school since she missed the bus. (no comma)

Punctuation Note:

The comma after the opening dependent clause is only used when the dependent clause is the *first* clause in the sentence. If the dependent clause comes second, no comma is needed. See the example in the second and third sentences above.

Compound-Complex Sentences

A compound-complex sentence consists of two or more independent clauses and at least one dependent clause. This type of sentence combines the features of compound and complex sentences. For example:

She wanted to go to the beach, but it was too cold, so she stayed home.

Note:

If you remove both the conjunctions in the example sentence above, you have three complete sentences. This is how you know you have a compound-complex sentence.

She wanted to go to the beach. It was too cold. She stayed home.

If you want your writing to look professional and not amateurish, you should vary your sentences between the sentence structures. Too many short choppy sentences or too many super long sentences can be off-putting for the reader.

Exercises:

1. What is a sentence?

  a) A group of letters

  b) A group of words that expresses a complete thought and contains a subject and a predicate

  c) A paragraph

  2. Which part of a sentence performs the action or is the focus of the sentence?

  a) Predicate

  b) Object

  c) Subject

  3. Which part of a sentence tells what the subject does or what is done to the subject?

  a) Predicate

  b) Object

  c) Subject

  4. What is a simple sentence?

  a) A sentence that contains one independent clause and expresses a complete thought

complete thought

  b) A sentence that contains two or more independent clauses joined by a conjunction or semicolon

  c) A sentence that contains one dependent clause

  5. What is a compound sentence?

  a) A sentence that contains one independent clause and one or more dependent clauses

  b) A sentence that contains two or more independent clauses joined by a conjunction or semicolon

  c) A group of words that does not express a complete thought

6. What is a dependent clause?

a) A group of words that contains a subject and a verb but cannot stand alone as a complete sentence

b) A sentence that contains one independent clause and one or more dependent clauses

c) A group of words that does not express a complete thought

7. What is a run-on sentence?

a) A sentence in which two or more independent clauses are improperly joined

b) A sentence that contains one independent clause and one or more dependent clauses

c) A group of words that does not express a complete thought

8. What is a fragment sentence?

a) A sentence in which two or more independent clauses are improperly joined

b) A group of words that does not express a complete thought and cannot stand alone as a sentence

c) A sentence that contains one dependent clause

9. What is a misplaced modifier?

a) A word or phrase that is in the wrong place in a sentence and creates confusion or ambiguity

b) A sentence in which two or more independent clauses are improperly joined

c) A sentence that contains one independent clause and one or more dependent clauses

10. What is a comma splice?

a) A sentence in which two or more independent clauses are improperly joined with a comma

b) A sentence that contains one dependent clause

c) A group of words that does not express a complete thought and cannot stand alone as a sentence

Chapter Fourteen

Punctuation and Mechanics

Finally, punctuation and mechanics are the finishing touches that give a sentence its polish and clarity. In this final basic grammar chapter, we'll explore the different types of punctuation, their functions, and the rules for using them correctly. We'll also discuss common errors and offer strategies for avoiding them.

Punctuation and mechanics are essential components of English grammar. They help us to convey meaning and clarify our writing. Consider "Let's eat grandma." Without the correct punctuation it seems this person is wanting to devour their grandma for dinner! "Let's eat, grandma." Tells the reader the person is beckoning for grandma to come have a meal.

Capitalization

Capitalization refers to the use of capital letters at the beginning of sentences, proper nouns, and the first letter of important words in titles. It is important to use capitalization correctly, as it can affect the meaning of a sentence. For example:

Incorrect: i went to the piggly wiggly.

Correct: I went to the Piggly Wiggly.

Punctuation Marks

Period (.) - The period is used to indicate the end of a sentence. It's sometimes called a full stop.

Question Mark (?) - The question mark is used to indicate a direct question.

Exclamation Mark (!) - The exclamation mark is used to indicate strong emotion or emphasis. One will suffice. Writing fourteen of them in a row really isn't necessary.

Comma (,) - The comma is used to separate items in a list, to separate clauses in a sentence, and to clarify meaning. Probably the most abused and wrongly used punctuation mark. I have tried to teach its usage throughout this book. The oxford comma is one of the main controversial topics in English grammar. The oxford comma is the comma right before the conjunction in a series: I like apples, bananas, (□the oxford comma) and oranges. I was taught when I was in school in the 1980s to leave it out. But, as an adult with an editor, I have been told to put it in! I personally say what does it hurt to just go ahead and include it? No one will count it wrong if you do, but they might count it wrong if you don't.

Semi-colon (;) - The semi-colon is used to separate two related independent clauses in a sentence. It is also used in a series where commas already exist. For example: I have visited Oklahoma City, Oklahoma; Austin, Texas; Kansas City, Kansas and New York, New York.

Colon (:) - The colon is used to introduce a list, a quote, or a summary. You can use it correctly be saying. I have a list of Halloween candies (and here they are) in place where the semicolon goes.

Apostrophe (') - The apostrophe is used to indicate possession or contraction.

Quotation Marks (" ") - Quotation marks are used to indicate a direct quote or to indicate that a word is being used in a specific sense. They are essential in creative writing to indicate dialogue.

Mechanics

Mechanics refer to the technical aspects of writing, such as spelling, grammar, and formatting. Mechanics are important but you need not worry about them until you are in the editing phase of your work.

Spelling - Correct spelling is important for clear communication. Spelling errors can change the meaning of a sentence and may cause confusion. The English language is full of homophones and homographs. I once used maul in place of maw when referring to a dragon. The first one, Maul is a hammer, the second is the mouth and snout of the dragon.

Grammar - Correct grammar is essential for clear and effective communication. Grammatical errors can change the meaning of a sentence and may affect the reader's understanding. This is where knowing the parts of speech and how they work comes into play. If you understand the parts of speech, you understand grammar.

Formatting - Correct formatting is important for clear and effective communication. This includes the use of margins, spacing, and font size. When writing an essay for example, one should not use frilly fonts or font sizes that are too big. This is why many English teachers give you the formatting instructions for a paper before you are assigned to write it.

Exercises:

1. What is the purpose of a comma?
a) To indicate a pause in speech
b) To separate items in a list
c) Both a and b
2. Which of the following is not a type of sentence ending punctuation?
a) Period
b) Comma
c) Exclamation point
3. When should a semicolon be used?
a) To separate items in a list
b) To join two independent clauses without a conjunction
c) To indicate a pause in speech
4. Which of the following is a correct way to use a colon?
a) Before a list
b) After a verb
c) Between a subject and a predicate
5. What is the purpose of quotation marks?
a) To indicate a pause in speech
b) To show a direct quote
c) To separate items in a list
6. Which of the following is not a type of dash?

a) En dash

b) Em dash

c) Hyphen

7. What is the purpose of an ellipsis?

a) To indicate a pause in speech

b) To show omission of words in a quote

c) To separate items in a list

8. What is the purpose of parentheses?

a) To show emphasis

b) To enclose additional information

c) Both a and b

9. What is the purpose of a hyphen?

a) To indicate a pause in speech

b) To connect two words

c) Both a and b

10. Which of the following is a correct way to use an apostrophe?

a) To form contractions

b) To show possession

c) Both a and b

11. Which of the following is a correct way to use capitalization?

a) To capitalize the first letter of every word in a sentence

b) To capitalize proper nouns and the first word of a sentence

c) To capitalize only the first word of a sentence

12. Which of the following is a correct way to use a question mark?

a) To end a declarative sentence

b) To end an interrogative sentence

c) To indicate excitement or emphasis

13. What is the purpose of a slash?

a) To indicate a pause in speech

b) To indicate a choice between two options

c) To separate items in a list

14. Which of the following is a correct way to use a bullet point?

a) To separate items in a list

b) To indicate emphasis

c) To show a quote

15. Which of the following is a correct way to use an exclamation point?

a) To end a declarative sentence

b) To end an interrogative sentence

c) To indicate excitement or emphasis

Chapter Fifteen

Verbals

Now, if you are happy with a basic grammar knowledge and you have reached this point, you are ready for some more advanced English grammar lessons. Advanced English grammar lessons begin now.

Verbals are words that look like verbs, but they function as different parts of speech in a sentence. It's like some verbs don't want to be verbs and instead want to be something else. There are three types of verbals: gerunds, participles, and infinitives. In this chapter, we will define each type of verbal, provide examples of how to use them correctly, and explain their roles in a sentence.

Gerunds

I have mentioned gerunds before. These are important to understand.

A gerund is a verbal that always ends in -ing and functions as a noun in a sentence, but it cannot be preceded by a helping verb. It can be the subject of a sentence, the object of a verb, or the object of a preposition. For example:

<u>Swimming</u> is good exercise. (subject of the sentence)

She loves <u>reading</u> books. (object of the verb "loves")

I am not good at <u>cooking</u>. (object of the preposition "at")

But not Jared is cooking us dinner. Because cooking has the helping verb is, it is actually a verb phrase "is cooking" and not a gerund.

If you ever take a test and see this question, you will understand why it's important to know what a gerund is:

Question: Which one of these words is a verb in this sentence. Choose all that apply.

Lying, stealing, and cheating are wrong.

1. lying

2. stealing

3. cheating

4. are

5. all of the above.

You might choose all of the above because they all look like verbs, but the answer is d) are. The others are all gerunds. In fact, lying, stealing, and cheating are the subjects of the sentence.

Participles

Participles are verbals that can function as adjectives in a sentence. In other words, they look like verbs but modify a noun like an adjective. There are two types of participles: present participles (-ing) and past participles (-ed or irregular). For example:

The <u>running</u> water is refreshing. (present participle as an adjective) running modifies/describes water.

The <u>broken</u> vase needs to be replaced. (past participle as an adjective) broken modifies/describes vase.

Don't dangle your participles.

Filled with deep potholes, the school bus driver drove down the road. This dangling participle makes it seem as if the school bus driver is filled with deep potholes instead of the road. Make the deep potholes point to the road not the driver. The school bus driver drove down a road filled with deep potholes.

Infinitives

An infinitive is a verbal formed by adding "to" before the base form of a verb (e.g., to eat, to run). It can function as a noun, an adjective, or an adverb in a sentence, but it's obviously not the main verb. For example:

To dance is my favorite hobby. (subject of the sentence)

She has a lot of work to do. (adjective modifying "work")

He stayed up late to finish his project. (adverb modifying "stayed up")

Split Infinitive:

My beloved Star Trek's opening monologue contains a split infinitive! To boldly go where no one has gone before. "To boldly go" is a split infinitive. It should be read "to go boldly" where no one has gone before. You are not supposed to put an adverb or anything between the infinitive "to" and its verb. If you do, you have a split infinitive. This used to be a big deal back in the olden days, but it's not that big of a thing anymore. Nowadays, I regularly see split infinitives in mainstream books.

Exercises:

1. Which of the following is NOT a type of verbal?

a) Infinitive

b) Gerund

c) Participle

d) Conjunction

2. What is the function of a gerund in a sentence?

a) To act as a verb

b) To act as an adjective

c) To act as an adverb

d) To act as a noun

3. Which of the following sentences contains a participle?

a) The boy who is running is fast.

b) Running is good exercise.

c) I am excited to see the movie.

d) The teacher handed out the graded papers.

4. In the sentence "I want to swim in the pool," what part of speech is "to swim"?

a) Gerund

b) Infinitive

c) Present participle

d) Past participle

5. Which of the following sentences contains a gerund phrase?

a) The book sitting on the table is mine.

b) She likes to read books in her free time.

c) Running shoes are essential for exercise.

d) The painting, created by a famous artist, sold for millions.

6. In the sentence "The bird flying overhead was a bald eagle," what part of speech is "flying"?

a) Gerund

b) Infinitive

c) Present participle

d) Past participle

7. Which of the following sentences contains an infinitive phrase?

a) He told a joke that was not funny.

b) The girl singing the solo has a beautiful voice.

c) To run a marathon, you need to train hard.

d) I am tired of listening to your excuses.

8. In the sentence "The dog, wagging its tail, ran to the door," what part of speech is "wagging"?

a) Gerund

b) Infinitive

c) Present participle

d) Past participle

9. Which of the following sentences contains a participial phrase?

a) She likes to ride her bike on the weekends.

b) The old man, walking slowly, crossed the street.

c) To write a good essay, you need to have a clear thesis statement.

d) The children were playing in the park.

10. What is the difference between a participle and a gerund?

a) A participle acts as a verb, while a gerund acts as an adjective or adverb.

b) A participle always ends in -ing, while a gerund can end in -ing or -ed.

c) A participle acts as an adjective or adverb, while a gerund acts as a noun.

d) A participle is used in the present tense, while a gerund is used in the past tense.

Chapter Sixteen

Transitive and Intransitive Verbs

In English grammar, verbs can be classified as either transitive or intransitive based on their usage in a sentence. Understanding the difference between these two types of verbs is essential for constructing grammatically correct sentences because being able to identify them will help with identifying direct and indirect objects.

Transitive Verbs

A transitive verb is a verb that requires a direct object to complete its meaning. The direct object is the person, place, thing, concept, or idea that receives the action of the verb. For example:

She ate an apple. (The apple is receiving the action of the verb ate. It's being eaten.)

He wrote a letter. (The letter is receiving the action of the verb wrote. It's being written.)

In both of these examples, the action of the verb (eating and writing) is directed towards a specific object (an apple and a letter).

Intransitive Verbs

An intransitive verb is a verb that does not require a direct object to complete its meaning. These verbs usually describe an action or a state of being that does not involve a specific recipient of the action. For example:

She sneezed loudly. (Nothing is receiving the action of the sneeze. This verb is intransitive.)

He slept all day. (Nothing is receiving the action of the verb slept. This verb is intransitive)

In both of these examples, the verbs do not have a specific object that receives the action. Instead, they describe an action or state of being without involving a direct recipient.

This lesson is easy, right. You can always figure out if the verb is transitive or intransitive, right? What about this sentence:

Ivan drove to the store.

Is drove transitive or intransitive? It's intransitive because the store is the object of a preposition and not a direct object receiving the action of drove.

What about this sentence?

Sally wrote a love note for Jeff.

If you said wrote is transitive, you're right. "for Jeff" is a prepositional phrase, but note is the direct object and is receiving the action of being written.

Transitive and intransitive verbs are important concepts in English grammar, and understanding their differences is essential for constructing grammatically correct sentences. Transitive verbs require a direct object to complete their meaning, while intransitive verbs do not. Be careful not to mistake objects of the preposition for direct objects. (for more about direct objects see chapter 18)

Exercises:

What is a transitive verb?

What is an intransitive verb?

How do you identify a transitive verb in a sentence?

How do you identify an intransitive verb in a sentence?

What is the difference between a direct object and an indirect object?

Can an intransitive verb have an object?

What is the role of a direct object in a sentence with a transitive verb?

What is the role of a subject in a sentence with an intransitive verb?

Can a verb be both transitive and intransitive?

How can you change a transitive verb into an intransitive verb?

Multiple Choice:

11. What is a transitive verb?

a) A verb that does not require an object

b) A verb that requires a direct object to complete its meaning

c) A verb that requires an indirect object to complete its meaning

12. What is an intransitive verb?

a) A verb that does not require an object

b) A verb that requires a direct object to complete its meaning

c) A verb that requires an indirect object to complete its meaning

13. Which of the following verbs is transitive?

a) Sleep

b) Run

c) Eat

14. Which of the following verbs is intransitive?

a) Hit

b) Laugh

c) Read

15. What is the role of a direct object in a sentence with a transitive verb?

a) It performs the action of the verb

b) It receives the action of the verb

c) It identifies the subject of the sentence

16. Can an intransitive verb have an object?

a) Yes, it always requires an object

b) No, it never requires an object

c) It depends on the context in which it is used

17. What is the role of a subject in a sentence with an intransitive verb?

a) It performs the action of the verb

b) It receives the action of the verb

c) It is the object of the verb

18. Can a verb be both transitive and intransitive?

a) Yes, depending on the context in which it is used

b) No, a verb can only be one or the other

c) It depends on whether it has a direct or indirect object

19. Which of the following sentences contains a transitive verb?

a) The sun rose early this morning.

b) The boy ran quickly to the store.

c) The teacher gave a quiz to the students.

20. How can you change a transitive verb into an intransitive verb?

a) By adding a direct object to the sentence

b) By removing the direct object from the sentence

c) By changing the verb tense

Chapter Seventeen

Predicate Adjectives and Predicate Nominatives

For verbs to be transitive they are usually action verbs, but what about verbs of being and linking verbs? Well, we have some ground to cover for verbs of being too. Predicate adjectives and predicate nominatives are two types of words that can be used in a sentence to describe the subject. In other words, these are adjectives or nouns that tell you something directly about the subject and are joined by linking verbs.

Predicate Adjectives

A predicate adjective is an adjective that follows a linking verb and tells something about the subject of the sentence. Linking verbs are verbs of being or verbs that have to do with the five senses, which can be action verbs or linking verbs. Linking verbs include "be," "seem," "appear," "taste," "look," and "become." For example:

The cake smells delicious.

(The linking verb is "smells," and "delicious" is the predicate adjective. You can tell "smells" is the linking verb and not an action verb because the subject "cake" is not doing the action of smelling. Don't let your desert smell you!)

She seems happy today.

(The linking verb is "seems," and "happy" is the predicate adjective. Seem is a vague verb but here it works. I would suggest you eliminate the verb "seem" in creative writing as much as possible. If it "seems" like a duck. It is indeed a duck! But, if you're not sure the person is actually happy like in the aforementioned sentence the verb "seem" works fine.)

In both of these examples, the predicate adjective follows a linking verb and describes the subject of the sentence (the cake and she, respectively).

Be careful: "That celebrity is a handsome man." Handsome is not a predicate adjective in this sentence because it's an adjective describing man and not celebrity. Man is the predicate nominative though.

Predicate Nominatives

A predicate nominative is a noun or pronoun that follows a linking verb and renames or identifies the subject of the sentence. You could also call it the predicate noun or pronoun if you are uncomfortable with nominative. "Nom" or "nominis" is Latin for "name". For example:

The winner of the race is John. (The "winner" is "John" John is the predicate nominative because "John" is renaming the "winner" which is the subject of the sentence.)

The new teacher is Mrs. Smith. (The "teacher" is "Mrs. Smith" Mrs. Smith is the predicate nominative because "Mrs. Smith" is renaming the "teacher" which is the subject of the sentence.)

In both of these examples, the predicate nominative follows a linking verb and renames or identifies the subject of the sentence (the winner and the new teacher, respectively).

Predicate adjectives and predicate nominatives are important components of English grammar. Predicate adjectives describe the subject of the sentence, while predicate nominatives rename or identify the subject of the sentence. Before you ask, yes, a sentence can have both a predicate adjective and predicate nominative.

Like this: Shirley is an engineer and is nice. Or Shirley is an engineer, and she is nice. Either way is fine. ("Engineer" is the P.N. and nice is the P.A.) Note: In the first sentence Shirley is both renamed and described. In the second sentence, which is a compound sentence, "Shirley" is renamed, and "she" is described. It's still one sentence but it has two clauses. See how useful knowing the difference between phrases and clauses can be!

Exercises:

1. Which of the following contains a predicate nominative?
   a.) The bird flew high.
   b.) The book is interesting.
   c.) The cat meowed loudly.

d.) The girl ran fast.

2. Which of the following contains a predicate adjective?

a.) The sun is bright.

b.) The dog barked loudly.

c.) The car drove quickly.

d.) The tree grew tall.

3. In the sentence "She looks tired," what is the predicate adjective?

a.) looks

b.) tired

c.) She

d.) In

4. In the sentence "He seems nice," what is the predicate adjective?

a.) seems

b.) He

c.) nice

d.) In

5. In the sentence "The cake tasted delicious," what is the predicate adjective?

a.) tasted

b.) delicious

c.) The cake

d.) In

6. In the sentence "My brother became a doctor," what is the predicate nominative?

a.) became

b.) My brother

c.) doctor

d.) In

7. In the sentence "The flowers smell sweet," what is the predicate adjective?

a.) smell

b.) sweet

c.) The flowers

d.) In

8. In the sentence "The soup is hot," what is the predicate adjective?

a.) is

b.) hot

c.) The soup

d.) In

9. In the sentence "The movie seemed boring," what is the predicate adjective?

a.) seemed

b.) boring

c.) The movie

d.) In

10. In the sentence "They appeared nervous," what is the predicate adjective?

a.) appeared

b.) nervous

c.) They

d.) In

Chapter Eighteen

Direct and Indirect Objects

Direct and indirect objects are two types of objects that can be used in a sentence to receive the action of the verb. Objects can be either nouns, pronouns, or even gerunds.

Direct Objects

A direct object is a noun or pronoun that directly receives the action of the verb. The direct object answers the question "What?" or "Whom?" after the verb. For example:

He kicked the ball. (The verb is "kicked," and "the ball" is the direct object. Kicked is transitive.)

She ate the sandwich. (The verb is "ate," and "the sandwich" is the direct object. Ate is transitive.)

In both of these examples, the direct object receives the action of the verb (kicked and ate).

Indirect Objects

An indirect object is a noun or pronoun that receives the direct object. The indirect object answers the question "To whom?" or "For whom?" after the verb. For example:

He gave the ball to his friend.

(The verb is "gave," "the ball" is the direct object, and "his friend" is the indirect object.) Because "friend" is the object of a preposition, it might be easier to see the indirect object if the sentence were written like this instead: **He gave his friend the ball.**

The ball was given. To whom was the ball given? (His friend.) Friend is the indirect object.

She bought a present for her sister.

(The verb is "bought," "a present" is the direct object, and "her sister" is the indirect object.) **She bought her sister a present.** The present was bought. For whom was the present bought? (Her sister) Sister is the indirect object.

In both of these examples, the indirect object receives the direct object (the ball and the present).

Direct and indirect objects are important components of English grammar. Direct objects receive the action of the verb, while indirect objects receive the direct object. If you can identify the direct object and then ask "to whom?" or "for whom?" and there is an answer in the sentence, that is the indirect object.

Exercises:

1. What is the direct object in the following sentence: "The dog chased the cat"?

a) dog

b) cat

c) chased

2. Which of the following sentences has an indirect object?

a) She bought a new car.

b) He gave the book to her.

c) They played soccer in the park.

3. What is the indirect object in the sentence: "The teacher gave the students a quiz"?

a) teacher

b) quiz

c) students

4. In the sentence "I wrote my mom a letter," what is the direct object?

a) wrote

b) mom

c) letter

5. What is the indirect object in the sentence: "She told me a secret"?

a) secret

b) me

c) told

6. Which of the following sentences has a direct object?

a) She danced all night.

b) He talked to his friend on the phone.

c) They went to the movies together.

7. What is the indirect object in the sentence: "He baked his mom a cake"?

a) mom

b) cake

c) baked

8. In the sentence "The doctor prescribed medication for her," what is the direct object?

a) prescribed

b) doctor

c) medication

9. What is the direct object in the sentence: "They watched a movie at the theater"?

a) watched

b) movie

c) theater

10. Which of the following sentences has both a direct and indirect object?

a) She read the book in one sitting.

b) He gave his sister a gift for her birthday.

c) They walked to the store and back.

Chapter Nineteen

Subject and Object Complements

Remember predicate adjectives and predicate nominatives? It turns out when you have something in the predicate telling you something about the subject, we have a name for that. It's called a complement. You can have a subject complement, or an object complement. (Compliment with an "I" would be like "You look nice today." Complement with an "E" means it goes together. It's complimentary. Like "That dress goes with your figure. The dress complements your figure.

Subject Complements

A subject complement is a word or phrase that follows a linking verb and describes or renames the subject of the sentence. Sound familiar?

Subject complements can be either predicate adjectives or predicate nominatives, which were covered in Chapter 17. For example:

My favorite color is blue. (The linking verb is "is," and "blue" is the predicate nominative that renames "my favorite color." Blue is the subject complement.)

She seems tired. (The linking verb is "seems," and "tired" is the predicate adjective that describes "she." Tired is the subject complement.)

In both of these examples, the subject complement follows a linking verb and describes or renames the subject of the sentence. Now on to newer territory.

Object Complements

An object complement is a word or phrase that follows a direct object and completes its meaning. Object complements can be either predicate adjectives or predicate nominatives. For example:

They painted the wall blue. (The direct object is "the wall," and "blue" is the object complement that describes it.)

The teacher considered him a genius. (The direct object is "him," and "a genius" is the object complement that renames him.)

In both of these examples, the object complement follows the direct object and completes its meaning.

This chapter probably could have been included in chapter 17, but I thought I would give you more practice with predicate nominative and predicate adjectives!

Exercises:

1. What is the subject complement in the sentence: "The cake smells delicious"?

a) cake

b) smells

c) delicious

2. Which of the following sentences has an object complement?

a) She ate a sandwich for lunch.

b) He painted the walls blue.

c) They went to the beach on vacation.

3. What is the object complement in the sentence: "She considered him her best friend"?

a) considered

b) friend

c) him

4. In the sentence "The teacher called her students intelligent," what is the subject complement?

a) called

b) teacher

c) intelligent

5. What is the object complement in the sentence: "He made his daughter a birthday cake"?

a) made

b) daughter

c) cake

6. Which of the following sentences has a subject complement?

a) She walked to the store.

b) He bought a new car.

c) They felt happy after the party.

7. What is the object complement in the sentence: "I consider traveling a learning experience"?

a) consider

b) traveling

c) experience

8. In the sentence "The doctor declared her healthy," what is the subject complement?

a) declared

b) doctor

c) healthy

9. What is the subject complement in the sentence: "The flowers looked beautiful in the sunlight"?

a) looked

b) flowers

c) beautiful

10. Which of the following sentences has both a subject and object complement?

a) She found the movie boring.

b) He gave his mom a bouquet of flowers.

c) They listened to music on the radio.

Indicative, Imperative, and Subjunctive Mood

The subjunctive mood is a verb form that expresses various states of unreality such as wishes, hypothetical situations, or doubts. In this chapter, we will define the subjunctive mood, provide examples of its use, and explain how it differs from the indicative mood. Finally, you will be able to easily tell if you should use "was" or "were" in a sentence. Once you understand subjunctive mood, you will never use "was" when you should have used "were" and vice versa again.

The Subjunctive Mood

The subjunctive mood is used to express hypothetical or unlikely situations, unreal conditions, wishes, doubts, or commands. It is often used in the context of an "if" or "wish" clause or to express uncertainty, possibility, or necessity. The subjunctive mood is formed differently depending on the verb tense, but it usually involves changing the form of the verb.

Here are some examples of the subjunctive mood in use:

If I were rich, I would travel the world. (The verb "were" is in the subjunctive mood, expressing an unreal situation. If it's wishful thinking use "were")

I wish I were a rich man. (If and wish are good indications you should use the verb were.

I was a rich man. (If it's a statement of fact use was instead.)

It is important that she be here on time. (The verb "be" is in the subjunctive mood, expressing necessity or obligation.)

I suggest that he go to the doctor. (The verb "go" is in the subjunctive mood, expressing a suggestion or recommendation.)

Differences between Subjunctive and Indicative Moods

The subjunctive mood differs from the indicative mood in that it expresses states of unreality, while the indicative mood expresses facts, actions, and events that are true or certain. For example:

If it rains, I will stay inside. (The verb "rains" is in the indicative mood, expressing a fact or likelihood.) Rain is forecasted or is possible.

I was a rich man. (The verb "was" is in the indicative mood, expressing a fact.)

If it were to rain, I would stay inside. (The verb "were" is in the subjunctive mood, expressing an unreal or hypothetical situation.) Rain is hypothetical. It may rain, it may not, no one has predicted it one way or the other.

Just remember to use "were" after "if" and "wish" if you are writing a sentence of wishful thinking, and use "was" when writing a sentence of fact and you will be fine. This will help in creative writing especially because it will help you discern between "were" and "was" more easily in most situations.

Exercises:

1. Which of the following sentences is in the indicative mood?

    A) I wish I could go to the concert.

    B) Go to the store and buy some milk.

    C) If I were you, I would take the job.

    D) Let's go to the beach this weekend.

2. Which of the following sentences is in the imperative mood?

    A) He asked if she wanted to go for a walk.

    B) Don't forget to turn off the lights.

    C) I wonder what time the movie starts.

    D) If only I had more free time.

3. Which of the following sentences is in the subjunctive mood?

    A) She runs five miles every day.

    B) If I had a million dollars, I would buy a mansion.

    C) I am going to the store.

    D) He always plays the guitar after dinner.

4. Which of the following sentences is in the indicative mood?

    A) I hope the weather is nice tomorrow.

    B) Be careful not to spill the coffee.

    C) If I were taller, I would play basketball.

    D) Let's have pizza for dinner tonight.

5. Which of the following sentences is in the imperative mood?

    A) I wonder what he will say.

B) Don't be late for your appointment.

C) If only I had studied more for the test.

D) She always reads a book before going to bed.

6. Which of the following sentences is in the subjunctive mood?

A) They are running in the park.

B) If he were here, he would help us.

C) I will call you later.

D) Let's go to the zoo this weekend.

7. Which of the following sentences is in the indicative mood?

A) It's important that you arrive on time.

B) Make sure you bring a jacket.

C) If only I had taken that job offer.

D) Let's practice our dance routine again.

8. Which of the following sentences is in the imperative mood?

A) I wonder what the score will be.

B) Don't forget to lock the door.

C) If only I had more money.

D) She always wears a hat when it's sunny.

9. Which of the following sentences is in the subjunctive mood?

A) We are planning a trip to Hawaii.

B) If she were here, she would know what to do.

C) I am going to the gym after work.

D) Let's watch a movie tonight.

10. Which of the following sentences is in the indicative mood?

A) It's great that you got the job.

B) Take out the garbage before you go.

C) If only I could travel the world.

D) Let's go for a walk in the park.

11. Which of the following sentences is in the imperative mood?

A) I wonder what the chef will prepare.

B) Don't touch the hot stove.

C) If only I had more time to read.

D) He always goes for a run in the morning.

12. Which of the following sentences is in the subjunctive mood?

A) She is studying for her exam.

B) If we had more supplies, we could finish the project.

C) I am meeting my friend for lunch.

D) Let's go to the beach this weekend.

Active and Passive Voice

Active and passive voice are two different ways of expressing the same idea in a sentence. Ah, the dreaded passive voice. Almost all creative writing advice tells you to avoid passive voice and always write in active voice, but is active voice always better in all situations?

Active Voice

In an active sentence, the subject of the sentence performs the action. Unless the sentence is inverted the subject is usually located at the beginning of the sentence, followed by a verb and an object. For example:

The cat chased the mouse. (The subject "cat" is actively chasing the object "mouse.")

In an active sentence, the subject is doing the action, which makes the sentence more direct and clearer.

Passive Voice

In a passive sentence, the object of the sentence becomes the subject, and the verb is changed to a form of "be" followed by the past participle of the verb. (The past participle form of the verb is the verb you use with helping verbs like have, has, or had. Like this: I *go* skiing a lot, I *went* skiing last week, I *have gone* skiing on many occasions. "Gone" is the past participle form of the verb "go.") For example:

The mouse *was chased* by the cat. (The object "mouse" becomes the subject, and the verb "chased" is changed to "was chased" to form the past participle form of the verb "chase" and therefore formed the passive sentence.)

In a passive sentence, the subject is receiving the action, which makes the sentence less direct and less clear. Passive voice is often used to shift the focus away from the person performing the action and onto the action itself.

Here are some more examples of active and passive voice:

Active voice: The chef cooked the meal.

Passive voice: The meal was cooked by the chef.

In the active sentence, the subject "chef" performs the action of cooking. In the passive sentence, the object "meal" becomes the subject, and the verb "cooked" is changed to "was cooked" to form the passive sentence.

Active voice: The car ran the red light.

Passive Voice: The red light was run by the car.

Starting to see the pattern yet? Let's look at another:

Active voice: The company hired a new employee.

Passive voice: A new employee was hired by the company.

In the active sentence, the subject "company" performs the action of hiring. In the passive sentence, the object "new employee" becomes the subject, and the verb "hired" is changed to "was hired" to form the passive sentence.

Sometimes you just have to use was and passive voice. You should never eliminate all passive voice, but you should have a small percentage compared to active voice when you edit. Probably no more than 5% of your entire essay, manuscript, or story. If your scene is set at a funeral, it would be silly to write: What a good friend was he, or What a good friend is he, or He is a good friend, when referring to the deceased. It would be: He was a good friend.

Consider:

Person 1: How did he die? Person 2: Friendly fire killed him. (Active)

Person 1: How did he die? Person 2: He was killed by friendly fire. (Passive)

It may be discouraged but sometimes it just looks, sounds, and reads better to use it anyway. But as you can see from the last example, it's also a matter of choice and opinion. Use passive voice sparingly and you will be fine.

Exercises:

1. Which of the following sentences is in active voice?

a) The cake was baked by my mom.

b) My mom baked the cake.

2. What is the passive voice form of the sentence "The teacher gave the students a test"?

a) The students were given a test by the teacher.

b) The teacher was giving the students a test.

3. In which of the following sentences is the subject in passive voice?

a) The cat chased the mouse.

b) The mouse was chased by the cat.

4. Which of the following sentences is in active voice?

a) The book was read by me.

b) I read the book.

5. What is the passive voice form of the sentence "They built a new house last year"?

a) A new house was built by them last year.

b) They were building a new house last year.

6. In which of the following sentences is the subject in passive voice?

a) The dog bit the mailman.

b) The mailman was bitten by the dog.

7. Which of the following sentences is in active voice?

a) The movie was watched by us.

b) We watched the movie.

8. What is the passive voice form of the sentence "She made a delicious cake"?

a) A delicious cake was made by her.

b) She was making a delicious cake.

9. In which of the following sentences is the subject in passive voice?

a) The teacher is teaching the lesson.

b) The lesson is being taught by the teacher.

10. Which of the following sentences is in active voice?

a) The song was sung by the choir.

b) The choir sang the song.

11. What is the passive voice form of the sentence "She wrote a book about her travels"?

a) A book about her travels was written by her.

b) She was writing a book about her travels.

12. In which of the following sentences is the subject in passive voice?

a) The baby is drinking the milk.

b) The milk is being drunk by the baby.

13. Which of the following sentences is in active voice?

a) The letter was written by my sister.

b) My sister wrote the letter.

14. What is the passive voice form of the sentence "He caught the ball"?

a) The ball was caught by him.

b) He was catching the ball.

15. In which of the following sentences is the subject in passive voice?

a) The chef is cooking the meal.

b) The meal is being cooked by the chef.

Chapter Twenty-Two

The Twelve Verb Tenses

Verbs are an essential part of every sentence. They indicate actions, events, or states of being. There are twelve verb tenses in the English language, and each of them has a specific purpose. Here we go with taking past, present, and future tenses and overcomplicating them! You're welcome!

Present Simple Tense

The present simple tense is used to describe actions that occur regularly or habits. It is also used to state facts or general truths. The present simple tense uses the base form of the verb.

Example: I play tennis every Monday.

Present Continuous Tense

The present continuous tense is used to describe actions that are currently happening or ongoing. It is formed by using the present tense of the verb 'to be' with the present participle form of the main verb. Continuous tense verbs always end in -ing.

Example: She is reading a book right now.

Present Perfect Tense

The present perfect tense is used to describe actions that occurred at an unspecified time in the past and have a connection to the present. It is formed by using the present tense of the verb 'to have' with the past participle form of the main verb. Most of the time perfect tense verbs end in -ed.

Example: I have lived in New York for five years.

Present Perfect Continuous Tense

The present perfect continuous tense is used to describe actions that started in the past and are still ongoing or have just stopped. It is formed by using the present tense of the verb 'to have' with 'been' and the present participle form of the main verb.

Example: They have been playing football for two hours.

Past Simple Tense

The past simple tense is used to describe actions that occurred at a specific time in the past. It is formed by using the past form of the main verb.

Example: She walked to the store yesterday.

Past Continuous Tense

The past continuous tense is used to describe actions that were ongoing at a specific time in the past. It is formed by using the past tense of the verb 'to be' with the present participle form of the main verb.

Example: I was eating dinner when she called.

Past Perfect Tense

The past perfect tense is used to describe actions that occurred before a specific time in the past. It is formed by using the past tense of the verb 'to have' with the past participle form of the main verb.

Example: They had finished their homework before they went to bed.

Past Perfect Continuous Tense

The past perfect continuous tense is used to describe actions that had been ongoing for a period of time before a specific time in the past.

It is formed by using the past tense of the verb 'to have' with 'been' and the present participle form of the main verb.

Example: I had been studying for hours before the exam.

Future Simple Tense

The future simple tense is used to describe actions that will occur in the future. It is formed by using the base form of the verb with 'will'.

Example: He will visit his grandparents next week.

Future Continuous Tense

The future continuous tense is used to describe actions that will be ongoing at a specific time in the future. It is formed by using the future tense of the verb 'to be' with the present participle form of the main verb. "Will" is still used and will always be used to indicate future tense in all its forms.

Example: I will be watching TV at eight o'clock tonight.

Future Perfect Tense

The future perfect tense is used to describe actions that will have been completed at a specific time in the future. It is formed by using the future tense of the verb 'to have' with the past participle form of the main verb.

Example: By next year, he will have graduated from college.

Future Perfect Continuous Tense

The future perfect continuous tense is a verb tense that is used to describe an ongoing action that will be completed at a specific time in the future. It is formed by using the auxiliary verb "will" or "shall" with "have been" and the present participle form of the main verb.

Example: By next year, I will have been studying for ten years.

In this example, the action of studying will have been ongoing for ten years by the time next year comes around. The future perfect continuous tense is used to emphasize the duration of an ongoing action up until a specific point in the future. It is commonly used to talk about actions that started in the past and are expected to continue into the future.

Example: By the time she retires, she will have been teaching for thirty years.

In this example, the action of teaching started in the past and is expected to continue up until the point when the speaker is referring to, which is the time when the woman retires. The future perfect continuous tense is often used in formal writing, such as academic or technical documents, to describe ongoing processes or activities that are expected to continue into the future.

Exercises:

1. Which tense is used to describe an action that will happen in the future?
   a) Present Perfect
   b) Future Simple

c) Past Continuous

d) Present Continuous

2. Which tense is used to describe an action that started in the past and continues up to the present?

a) Past Simple

b) Present Continuous

c) Present Perfect Continuous

d) Present Perfect

3. Which tense is used to describe an action that was completed at a specific time in the past?

a) Present Perfect

b) Past Continuous

c) Past Simple

d) Future Simple

4. Which tense is used to describe an action that started and finished in the past?

a) Present Perfect Continuous

b) Past Simple

c) Past Perfect

d) Future Simple

5. Which tense is used to describe an action that will be ongoing at a future time?

a) Present Continuous

b) Future Continuous

c) Past Perfect Continuous

d) Present Perfect Continuous

6. Which tense is used to describe an action that happened before another action in the past?

a) Past Simple

b) Past Perfect

c) Future Simple

d) Present Perfect

7. Which tense is used to describe an action that is happening right now?

a) Present Perfect Continuous

b) Present Continuous

c) Past Continuous

d) Past Perfect Continuous

8. Which tense is used to describe an action that will have been completed by a certain time in the future?

a) Present Perfect

b) Past Simple

c) Future Perfect

d) Past Perfect Continuous

9. Which tense is used to describe an action that had been completed before another action in the past?

a) Present Perfect Continuous

b) Past Perfect

c) Future Simple

d) Present Simple

10. Which tense is used to describe an action that will have been ongoing for a certain amount of time by a future time?

a) Present Continuous

b) Future Perfect Continuous

c) Past Simple

d) Past Perfect Continuous

11. Which tense is used to describe an action that is expected to happen in the near future?

a) Future Simple

b) Present Perfect

c) Past Continuous

d) Present Simple

12. Which tense is used to describe an action that is habitually done in the past?

a) Past Simple

b) Past Continuous

c) Past Perfect

d) Past Perfect Continuous

13. Which tense is used to describe an action that was ongoing in the past but was interrupted by another action?

a) Present Perfect Continuous

b) Past Perfect Continuous

c) Past Continuous

d) Present Continuous

14. Which tense is used to describe an action that had been completed before a specific time in the past?

a) Past Perfect

b) Present Perfect

c) Future Simple

d) Present Simple

15. Which tense is used to describe an action that will be completed at a specific time in the future?

a) Present Perfect

b) Future Simple

c) Past Simple

d) Present Simple

And there you have it! You have reached the end of the book. I think I have covered about everything you need to write, read, and understand English grammar and composition in any medium, but I welcome questions and comments. If there is anything you are confused with or need clarification on, send me an email at cleavebourb on@gmail.com and I will get back with you. If there is anything about English grammar I didn't cover, but you want to know about let me know and I will not only answer you on the subject, but I will add it to this book. Thanks for everything! The next section contains the answer keys. I hope you did well on all the exercises!

Chapter Twenty-Three

Answers Keys to Exercises

Chapter 1 Sentence Types Exercises Answer Key:

1. Answer: a
2. Answer: c
3. Answer: a
4. Answer: d
5. Answer: b
6. Answer: b
7. Answer: c
8. Answer: a
9. Answer: d
10. Answer: d
11. Answer: c

12. Answer: d

13. Answer: a

14. Answer: a

15. Answer: b

Chapter 2 Phrases and Clauses Exercises Answer Key:

1. Answer: b

2. Answer: b

3. Answer: a

4. Answer: b

5. Answer: c

6. Answer: b

7. Answer: a

8. Answer: a

9. Answer: b

10. Answer: b

Chapter 3 Nouns Exercises Answer Key:

1. A common noun is a noun that refers to a general or non-specific person, place, thing, or idea, such as "dog," "chair," or "idea."

2. A proper noun is a specific name of a person, place, or thing, such as "John," "Paris," or "Nike."

3. An abstract noun is a noun that refers to an intangible concept or idea, such as "love," "happiness," or "justice."

4. A concrete noun is a noun that refers to a tangible object or physical thing, such as "table," "tree," or "car."

5. A collective noun is a noun that refers to a group of people, animals, or things, such as "family," "herd," or "team."

6. A countable noun is a noun that can be counted and has a singular and plural form, such as "book" and "books."

7. A non-countable noun is a noun that cannot be counted and only has a singular form, such as "water," "money," or "advice."

8. A compound noun is a noun made up of two or more words that function as a single unit, such as "toothbrush," "laptop," or "sunflower."

9. A possessive noun is a noun that shows ownership or possession, such as "John's car" or "the company's profits."

10. A singular noun is a noun that refers to one person, place, thing, or idea, such as "book," "chair," or "idea."

11. A plural noun is a noun that refers to more than one person, place, thing, or idea, such as "books," "chairs," or "ideas."

Chapter 4 Noun Phrases Exercises Answer Key:

1. A noun phrase is a group of words that includes a noun and any modifiers that describe or identify it.

2. The function of a noun phrase in a sentence is to act as the

subject, object, or complement of a verb, or to serve as a modifier of another noun or noun phrase.

3. An appositive phrase in a noun phrase is a noun or noun phrase that renames or explains another noun or noun phrase in the sentence.

4. A relative clause in a noun phrase is a clause that begins with a relative pronoun and describes or identifies the noun or pronoun in the noun phrase.

5. A post-modifier in a noun phrase is a word or phrase that comes after the head noun and provides additional information about it.

6. A pre-modifier in a noun phrase is a word or phrase that comes before the head noun and provides additional information about it.

7. A noun clause in a noun phrase is a clause that functions as a noun and is introduced by a subordinating conjunction.

8. A complement in a noun phrase is a word or phrase that follows the head noun and provides additional information about it, such as an adjective or a noun clause.

9. A head noun in a noun phrase is the main noun that the phrase is referring to and all other modifiers and phrases in the noun phrase are describing or identifying it.

Chapter 5 Verbs Exercises Answer key:

1. Answer: b

2. Answer: c

3. Answer: c

4. Answer: a

5. Answer: a

6. Answer: a

7. Answer: c

8. Answer: c

9. Answer: a

10. Answer: c

Chapter 6 Pronouns Exercises Answer keys:

1. Answer: c

2. Answer: c

3. Answer: d

4. Answer: a

5. Answer: d

6. Answer: d

7. Answer: d

8. Answer: a

9. Answer: b

10. Answer: c

11. Answer: a

12. Answer: a

13. Answer: c

14. Answer: c

15. Answer: a

Pronoun case and perspective Answers:

1.Answer: The subjective (nominative) case of pronouns is used as the subject of a sentence. Examples include: I, you, he, she, it, we, they.

2. Answer: The objective case of pronouns is used as the object of a verb or preposition. Examples include: me, you, him, her, it, us, them.

3. Answer: The possessive case of pronouns shows ownership or possession. Examples include: my, your, his, hers, its, our, their.

4. Answer: First-person perspective uses pronouns like "I" and "we" to refer to oneself or oneself and others. Second-person perspective uses pronouns like "you" to refer to the person being spoken to. Third-person perspective uses pronouns like "he," "she," and "they" to refer to someone or something that is not the speaker or the person being spoken to.

5. Answer: You should determine the appropriate pronoun case and perspective by identifying the role of the pronoun in the sentence (subject, object, possessive), and by considering the perspective from which the sentence is being written (first-person, second-person, third-person). Additionally, it is important to consider the context of the sentence and the intended meaning.

Chapter 7: Adjective and Adverbs Exercises Answer Key:

1. Answer: b red

2. Answer: b well

3. Answer: b green

4. Answer: b quickly

5. Answer: b ugly

6. Answer: b easily

7. Answer: b brow

8. Answer: b carefully

9. Answer: b old

10. Answer: b slowly

11. Answer: b friendly

12. Answer: a beautiful

13. Answer: a hard

14. Answer: d easily

15. Answer: b hot

16. Answer: b honestly

17. Answer: b new

18. Answer: b quickly

19. Answer: b cold

20. Answer: d well

Chapter 8: Adjective and Adverb Phrases Exercises Answer Key:

1. Answer: b A group of words that modify a noun or pronoun

2. Answer: b A group of words that modify a verb, adjective, or another adverb

3. Answer: b The car with the broken window

4. Answer: c The dog barked loudly

5. Answer: b To modify a noun or pronoun

6. Answer: b To modify a verb, adjective, or another adverb

7. Answer: a Yes

8. Answer: a Yes

9. Answer: b An adjective phrase modifies a noun or pronoun, while an adverb phrase modifies a verb, adjective, or another adverb.

10. Answer: b No

11. Answer: b No

12. Answer: a Yes

13. Answer: a Yes

14. Answer: a Yes

15. Answer: a Yes

Chapter 9: Prepositions Exercises Answer Key:

1. Prepositions:

1.Answer: A

2. Answer: C

3. Answer: B

4. Answer: C

5. Answer: C

6. Answer: A

7. Answer: B

8. Answer: A

9. Answer: A

10. Answer: A

Prepositions and Antecedents:

1.Answer: B

2. Answer: C

3. Answer: A

4. Answer: D

5. Answer: D

6. Answer: C

7. Answer: D

8. Answer: D

9. Answer: B

Chapter 10: Conjunctions Exercises Answer Key:

Coordinating Conjunctions:

1.Answer: c) and

2. Answer: b) but

3. Answer: c) or

4. Answer: d) for

5. Answer: d) so

6. Answer: d) if

7. Answer: a) and

8. Answer: d) as

9. Answer: d) yet

10. Answer: d) for

Subordinating Conjunctions:

1.Answer: B

2. Answer: B

3. Answer: C

4. Answer: A

5. Answer: C

6. Answer: B

7. Answer: C

8. Answer: B

9. Answer: A

10. Answer: D

Correlative Conjunctions:

1.Answer: C

2. Answer: C

3. Answer: D

4. Answer: A

5. Answer: D

Chapter 11: Interjections Exercises Answer Key:

1. b

2. b

3. c

4. b

5. b

6. b

7. b

8. b

9. b

10. b

11. b

12. a

13. **b**

14. **a**

15. **b**

Chapter 12 Articles Exercises Answer Key:

1. d

2. b

3. c

4. a

5. c

6. d

7. b

8. b

9. b

10. c

11. c

12. b

13. c

14. b

15. b

Chapter 13: Sentence Structure Exercises Answer Key:

1. Answer: b

2. Answer: c

3. Answer: a

4. Answer: a

5. Answer: b

6. Answer: a

7. Answer: a

8. Answer: b

9. Answer: a

10. Answer: a

Chapter 14: Punctuation and Mechanics Exercises Answer Key:

1. Answer: c

2. Answer: b

3. Answer: b

4. Answer: a

5. Answer: b

6. Answer: c

7. Answer: b

8. Answer: c

9. Answer: b

10. Answer: c

11. Answer: b

12. Answer: b

13. Answer: b

14. Answer: a

15. Answer: c

Chapter 15: Verbals Exercises Answer Key:

1. Answer: d Conjunction

2. Answer: d To act as a noun

3. Answer: a The boy who is running is fast.

4. Answer: b Infinitive

5. Answer: c Running shoes are essential for exercise.

6. Answer: c Present participle

7. Answer: c To run a marathon, you need to train hard.

8. Answer: c Present participle

9. Answer: b The old man, walking slowly, crossed the street.

10. Answer: c A participle acts as an adjective or adverb, while a gerund acts as a noun.

Chapter 16: Transitive and Intransitive Verbs Exercises Answer Key:

1. A transitive verb is a verb that requires a direct object to complete its meaning.

2. An intransitive verb is a verb that does not require a direct object to complete its meaning.

3. A transitive verb can be identified by looking for a verb that has a direct object following it in the sentence.

4. An intransitive verb can be identified by looking for a verb that does not have a direct object following it in the sentence.

5. A direct object is a noun or pronoun that receives the action of a transitive verb, while an indirect object is a noun or pronoun that receives the direct object of the transitive verb.

6. No, an intransitive verb cannot have an object.

7. The direct object in a sentence with a transitive verb receives the action of the verb and answers the question "what?" or "whom?"

8. The subject in a sentence with an intransitive verb performs the action of the verb and answers the question "who?" or "what?"

9. Yes, some verbs can be both transitive and intransitive, depending on the context in which they are used.

10. To change a transitive verb into an intransitive verb, you can remove the direct object from the sentence.

Multiple Choice:

1. Answer: b

2. Answer: a

3. Answer: c

4. Answer: b

5. Answer: b

6. Answer: b

7. Answer: a

8. Answer: a

9. Answer: c

10. Answer: b

Chapter 17: Predicate Adjectives and Predicate Nominatives Exercises Answer Key:

1. Answer: b. The book is interesting.

2. Answer: a. The sun is bright.

3. Answer: b. tired

4. Answer: c. nice

5. Answer: b. delicious

6. Answer: c. doctor

7. Answer: b. sweet

8. Answer: b. hot

9. Answer: b. boring

10. Answer: b. nervous

Chapter 18: Direct and Indirect Objects Exercises Answer Key:

1. Answer: b cat

2. Answer: b He gave the book to her.

3. Answer: c students

4. Answer: c letter

5. Answer: b me

6. Answer: b He talked to his friend on the phone.

7. Answer: a mom

8. Answer: c medication

9. Answer: b movie

10. Answer: b He gave his sister a gift for her birthday.

Chapter 19: Subject and Object Complements Exercises Answer Key:

1. Answer: c delicious

2. Answer: b He painted the walls blue.

3. Answer: b friend

4. Answer: c intelligent

5. Answer: c cake

6. Answer: c They felt happy after the party.

7. Answer: b traveling

8. Answer: c healthy

9. Answer: c beautiful

10. Answer: a She found the movie boring.

Chapter 20: Indicative, Imperative, and Subjunctive Mood Exercises Answer Key:

1. Answer: a

2. Answer: b

3. Answer: b

4. Answer: a

5. Answer: b

6. Answer: b

7. Answer: a

8. Answer: b

9. Answer: b

10. Answer: b

11. Answer: b

12. Answer: b

Chapter 21: Active and Passive Voice Exercises Answer Key:

1. Answer: b My mom baked the cake.

2. Answer: a The students were given a test by the teacher.

3. Answer: b The mouse was chased by the cat.

4. Answer: b I read the book.

5. Answer: b The mailman was bitten by the dog.

6. Answer: b We watched the movie.

7. Answer: a A delicious cake was made by her.

8. Answer: b The lesson is being taught by the teacher.

9. Answer: b The choir sang the song.

10. Answer: a A book about her travels was written by her.

11. Answer: b The milk is being drunk by the baby.

12. Answer: b My sister wrote the letter.

13. Answer: a The ball was caught by him.

14. Answer: b The meal is being cooked by the chef.

Chapter 22: The Twelve Verb Tenses Exercises Answer Key:

1. Answer: b Future Simple

2. Answer: c Present Perfect Continuous

3. Answer: c Past Simple

4. Answer: b Past Simple

5. Answer: b Future Continuous

6. Answer: b Past Perfect

7. Answer: b Present Continuous

8. Answer: c Future Perfect

9. Answer: b Past Perfect

10. Answer: b Future Perfect Continuous

11. Answer: a Future Simple

12. Answer: a Past Simple

13. Answer: c Past Continuous

14. Answer: a Past Perfect

15. Answer: b Future Simple

Also By Cleave Bourbon

Tournament of Mages Series:

Red Mage: Ascending Book 1

Blue Mage: Equinox Book 2

Black Mage: Cursed Book 3

Green Mage: Metamorphosis Book 4

Grey Mage: Protector Book 5

White Mage: Rhapsody Book 6

Enter the Arena Book 7

Prequel The Seventh God

Shadows of the First Trine Series:

Book 1 The Harrowing Path

Book 2 Serpent in the Mist

Book 3 Seer of Shadows

Book 4 Undead Inheritance

Book 5 Fury of the Lich

Prequel Shadows of Yesterday

War of the Oracle Series:

Dragon's Blood Book 1

The Cursed Phylactery Book 2

Wizards of War Book 3

Lurker in the Shadows Book 4

About the Author

Cleave Bourbon is a native of Texas. His Texas heritage and his love of science fiction and fantasy allows him to write weird westerns among other fantastical stories. In fact, he has loved all things fantasy since he read the Belgariad by David and Leigh Eddings in High School. He says the word "fantasy" comes from fantasizing, so the sky is the limit on what fantasy can encompass as far as writing goes, so he isn't afraid to experiment and write new twists to liven up old tropes. Being that he holds both a B.A. and an M.A. in English, he writes full time and teaches in his spare time. He teaches Junior High and High School level grammar, vocabulary, and writing online. He says he will never stop writing and he will never stop teaching, unless he becomes physically unable to do so. He currently resides in Texas with his Tortoise Shell Cat, Khaleesi.

www.ingramcontent.com/pod-product-compliance
Lightning Source LLC
Chambersburg PA
CBHW031330060726
47590CB00007B/2418